Technology Integration Ac
Parent Resource for Virtua

By Scott Paulson

Copyright 2021 Scott F. Paulson

All Rights Reserved. No part of this book may be reproduced or utilized in any form or by any means electronic or mechanical, recording, or by any information storage and retrieval system, without permission in writing from the publisher.

Dedication

To educators who strive to provide the best instruction for their students.

Table of Contents

About the Author

Introduction

English: Reading

English: Writing

Math

Science

Health

History and Current Events

Geography

Foreign Language

Music and Song

Technology and Computers

More

About the Author

Scott Paulson is an award winning, Midwestern American English teacher who received a Bachelor of Arts degree and an Illinois teaching certificate to teach language arts to secondary learners. He earned his Bachelor's Degree at North Central College in Naperville, Illinois, after which he acquired more than 40 hours of college and university credits in computer-related education and Spanish language courses. Of relevance to the content of this book, his many teaching awards include numerous "Larry Stilgebauer Award of Excellence" honors for excellent use of integrated technology in the classroom. During his more than four decades of teaching, he spent fifteen years integrating computer use across the curriculum in public middle schools and community colleges in the Chicago area.

As it happened, the school for which he taught middle school received a grant for a computer lab. The principal needed a teacher to take charge of the computer lab. Having been appropriately educated for such a position, Paulson was selected to teach students in the new lab. The challenge for him was having no curriculum or textual materials for an academically integrated computer lab. He had the task of setting up the lab during the summer months before it opened, as well as creating the curriculum and developing the materials to be used in the new classes. From the beginning, he has continually developed many lesson plans and materials for his students to learn language arts, mathematics, economics, science, health, history, current events, English as a Second Language, Spanish, computer skills, keyboarding, and internet usage. Additionally, he has continued taking classes to learn more regarding the integration of academic subject matter with technology. He has been called upon repeatedly to train fellow educators regarding the integration of technology across the curriculum. He has consistently received excellent ratings for his teaching abilities by his superiors throughout the years.

The principals for whom he worked always wanted every student in the school to spend time in the integrated computer lab at some point during the school year. Therefore, as well as the general education students who filed through his classroom, he also taught the gifted, the special education, the bilingual, and the handicapped students who were incorporated into his classes at various times throughout the day. At one point, some of his classes had as many as 40 students in a class period. Naturally, due to the differences in student population, lessons that could challenge the most advanced students while being appropriate for limited learners had to be developed. His appropriate and necessary pairing of students at the computers assisted with mentorships. After all, the lab had 25 computers versus 40 students in some class periods. Fortunately, the periods when special education and handicapped students were in the lab, a teacher's aide sometimes accompanied the students.

With the addition of a bilingual population in Paulson's classes, he taught many Spanish-speaking students who were learning English in developmental English classes as well as in English as a Second Language classes. Consequently, he registered for the Spanish language program at the College of DuPage in Glen Ellyn, Illinois, and completed all of the courses. The knowledge obtained in the classes enabled him to communicate with and relate to the bilingual population of students effectively. As he learned Spanish, he noticed the many similarities between English and Spanish and documented them in detail. He also documented the differences between Spanish and English that made learning Spanish challenging. He has shared his knowledge of the similarities and differences between the English and Spanish languages with his students. This educational information is in his book titled *English and Spanish: The Similarities and Differences (Including an Extensive Grammar and Phonics Review)*.

After teaching middle school-aged students for 34 years in Joliet, Illinois, Paulson continually integrates technology in developmental English and English as a Second Language classes he has taught at community colleges in the Chicago area.

Introduction

The progression of online teaching of subject matter across the academic curriculum's spectrum, which began in the 1990s, has peaked during 2020's pandemic. With socially distanced learning and virtual learning becoming the normal, educators' sharing of creative and beneficial lessons with one another has become more necessary. This book's creation has been inspired by the need for educators to assist fellow-educators and parents in successfully educating students through trying times and beyond.

On the following pages, there are lessons and lesson ideas for teachers and parents to teach and for students to learn through technology. By using a computer's Internet and the various applications that are available on a computer, the following lesson plans and detailed lessons will assist educators and parents in teaching students necessary computer and keyboarding skills while integrating English, reading, writing, editing, and comprehension, as well as math, science, economics, government, geography, history, current events, and more.

Altering lessons to meet each student's specific needs and differing academic levels is necessary for meeting every student's academic goals and objectives. These lessons and teaching ideas will guide educators and parents to produce activities that teach and motivate students.

Each chapter begins with general activities that can be adapted by educators. Besides general lessons and activity ideas, most chapters have specific lessons and activities for educators to use. Find the lessons and activities that are suitable for your teaching situation and your students. Alter them as needed, and then incorporate them into your lessons, whether the instruction is administered onsite or virtually. Enhance the methods and lessons with your own creativity, and then share the teaching methods and activities that work best with others.

English: Reading

Reading comprehension is an objective that should be used cautiously when taught through online materials. Finding appropriate reading material in terms of content, reading level, and student interest can be a challenge for educators. Though it should be understood, before assigning a reading assignment via technology, scrutinize the entire document. Online written reviews of the reading material and any comments about the reading selection, if any are available, may be assistive in deciding the content's appropriateness for students.

Check the reading level. If a reading level is not available, as it most often is not for online writings, there are ways in which a text's reading level can be determined. One way to determine the reading level of material is to put the text, or a portion of a lengthy text, into a word processor in which the reading level of text is calculated. I use Microsoft Word.

Specifically, highlight the text on the Internet and then 'cut and paste' it into a new Word document. To find the reading level of a document in Microsoft Word, do the following: click on the File tab in the upper left-hand corner of the screen; in the drop-down menu, click on Options; then click on Proofing; find the section that reads "When correcting spelling and grammar in Word," check the box in front of "Show readability statistics." Then, do a "Spelling & Grammar" check. To do a Spelling and Grammar check, with the document still open in Microsoft Word, click on the Review tab above the document. Below the File tab on the far left, there is an option reading "ABC Spelling & Grammar." Click on it and do the spelling and grammar check. If this produces stops at spelling and grammar errors that are in the document, quickly click "ignore" or "ignore all" which is found on the right side of the screen. When the spelling and grammar check is completed, a box will appear that gives the Flesch-Kincaid Reading Level, as well as other information about the text. Again, there are other methods of determining the reading levels of texts.

When you have noted and documented the readability level and possibly other information that you want to know about the text, click out of the document without saving it, as it is possible that the reading material you are going to have your students read online is copyrighted and the duplication of the material may not be legal. In other words, have students read what is on the computer screen as opposed to mass-producing the text if it may not or is not legal to make copies of it.

…

"Book Report Assignment"

Student Instructions: After reading a book approved by your teacher for the book report assignment, write a report.

Write the report in paragraphs, in which the first paragraph introduces your report. The introduction should have the main idea of the story, including the title, author, publisher, and most recent copyright date of the book.

The second paragraph should concentrate on the setting and important characters in the story. The setting is the location and time period in which the story occurs. The characters named in your report should include the main characters. Tell something about each character who is included.

The third paragraph should be about the plot, in which you explain what the major characters do or attempt to do in the story. Depending on the story, this is where you could write about any problems or concerns the characters encounter in the story. If characters' problems are solved within the story, include the solutions to their problems in the plot paragraph.

The fourth paragraph should be your report's conclusion, in which you write your reactions to the book. You could answer the following questions in your conclusion: Did you like reading the book? Tell why you did or didn't enjoy reading it. Would you recommend this book for others to read? Tell why you would or would not recommend it. Why, in your opinion, did the author write this book? How were the main characters good or bad people? Did the story teach a lesson of some sort? If so, what is the lesson?

Finally, if you encountered new words while reading this book, please list them as "New Words" at the end of your report.

Write your report in Microsoft Word, using the Times New Roman font at 12 characters per inch, and save it to your English folder as: (YourName/ClassPeriodNumber/BookReport). Remember to put your name, your class period number, and the due date of the assignment in the upper left-hand corner.

…

"Create a Crossword Puzzle Assignment"

After the class reads a book together, have the students create a crossword puzzle, with the clues and answers being about the book's content. Crosswords are a good activity for learning vocabulary, too. I have used the "Expert Crosswords and More" software, inexpensively available on Amazon. Additionally, WordMint.com is one of the websites that allows a computer user to make an account for creating crosswords. An email address is needed in order to create an account.

To introduce crossword creations to the class, create one for the students on any topic of which they are familiar, such as a novel or short story the entire class has previously read, their school, popular entertainers, whatever. As students see the creation, they learn that every term or word (that is an answer on the puzzle) has a clue (that is listed below the crossword puzzle's grid.) Crossword creation programs usually have a well-designed section where the puzzle creator can easily enter the words and clues for the puzzle. Then, with a click of the mouse as instructed by the program, the crossword puzzle is created.

Create a crossword with the students and, if possible, display the process on a large screen that the entire class can see. Ask the students for topic suggestions and choose one of them. Then have the students provide the words or terms to be typed in the program. Next, have the students offer the clues, which are then typed in. Show the puzzle that the class created together, and then have the students create one of their own. Again, it is a great follow-up after the students have read a novel.

Note to educators: Naturally, crossword creations can be used in other academic areas, such as science, history, health, and geography, as well as in current events. Give the students a theme or topic when making the assignment. Print out and distribute the best student crossword puzzle creations to be solved by the class, as it is motivational for them to produce their best work. Additionally, you might want to have students who have difficulty with the assignment discreetly teamed up with a partner to serve as a mentor.

…

"Create a Word Search Assignment"

Create a word search with vocabulary or other words related to a novel being read in class. Once again, there are many websites in which word searches can be created, including WordMint.com. Of course, simply using lined graph paper and a pencil is a possible method of creating a word search, too. Like the crossword puzzles discussed previously, word searches can be created for other subject areas, as well.

…

"Vocabulary Enrichment Assignment"

After students have created an email account for class and school use, students can subscribe for Merriam-Webster's "Word of the Day" to receive a new vocabulary word every day. Merriam-Webster's webpage is located online at "https://www.merriam-webster.com/word-of-the-day/calendar."

On the webpage, scroll down a short distance to where one sees the text, "Learn a new word every day. Delivered to your inbox!" In the box following this text, one enters his or her email address and clicks "Subscribe."

As an occasional vocabulary assignment, have students read recent "Word of the Day" emails that they have received. Written assignments can include activities such as writing original sentences in which vocabulary words received from Merriam-Webster in emails are inserted into the sentences. Additionally, have students create a folder, possibly labeled "Dictionary," within their email accounts so that they can move the "Word of the Day" emails to the folder for organizational purposes as well as for easy access when needed.

…

A poster on my classroom wall says, "Learn to Read – Read to Learn!"

Educators often post, and are often required to post, student goals and objectives for learning. It is good to remind students the benefits of learning.

Remind students the benefits of learning to read, which include: the more a person reads, the better a reader he or she becomes; reading improves writing abilities; reading improves vocabulary; reading can give information; reading can entertain; reading can make a person feel better by reducing stress and depression; reading can increase imagination; reading can help one remember and be focused; and, reading exercises one's brain to help avoid serious illnesses later in life.

English: Writing

When a student practices writing, his or her writing skills are promoted. Therefore, the more assignments involving writing, the more advantageous the activities are for the student's learning. Beyond the norm of assigning short essays, an educator can assign students many other assignments that keep them writing on a daily basis.

At the beginning of the school year, students can write an introduction of themselves. This is followed by the teacher introducing himself or herself, and then having the students read or discuss their own introductions to the class. Another form of this activity, which I like even better, is pairing students up and letting them talk to one another for approximately 15 minutes. During this time, the students introduce themselves to their partner and learn some things about one another. After this, each student writes an introduction of the student with whom he or she had spoken. In the future, the writer of each introduction reads his or her short introduction of the student to the class. This allows the class members to get to know their classmates and hopefully to start friendships within the class.

…

"Personal Journal Assignment"

Once a week, usually on Fridays, I have students spend 5 minutes or so writing in their Personal Journal. The agreement is that the students' personal journals are kept private. They know I am watching them as they write in their Journal, as I need to give a participation grade determined by their willingness to write. In time, journal writing often becomes one of their favorite activities in my classes. In fact, it is sometimes challenging to get some students to stop writing so the class can move on to other class' activities. They keep their journals on their flash drives, though they kept them on floppy disks when I started doing this activity back in the day. They keep their saved computer class work on a flash drive much as they keep their other classes' assignments in a notebook. By not saving their personal journal to the school's computers or the school's network, there is little chance of anyone else seeing their private writings. The objective of such journal writing is to get students to write freely and uninhibitedly. Again, practicing writing is beneficial to them.

This personal journal writing can be assigned during virtual and in-class computer-based learning. If a teacher or parent intends to read the content of everything a student writes, be sure the student is aware so they can monitor their own content for the public viewing, as many students consider their personal journals equate to a diary of sorts. The times a student wants a personal journal entry to be read, show interest without being judgmental or critical. Yet, point out written errors to keep the process educational as one would when reviewing any other written assignments with a student.

…

Other writing assignments include the writing of book reports on the computer, which was detailed in the "English: Reading" section. I often mention a current event of which I believe my students are interested or need to be informed. Following the sharing of information, there may be student questions or comments. The writing assignment attempts to engage the students in writing their reactions or opinions about the current event. Many times, a current topic is a two-sided governmental or political issue. In these instances, students are asked to side with one side of the issue. Then they are instructed to support their opinions. In current times as I am organizing this book, appropriate topics can be centered within the pandemic-related issues confronting people. Pandemic writing topics can logically be about the debates regarding the public's need to wear masks as well as the debates about the closures of businesses, churches, and schools. Students can write reasoned opinions about whether or not they believe they should be learning virtually from home, learning in school, or a combination of the two venues.

Such writing assignments can be evaluated for the students' abilities to write properly at the computer in terms of content, spelling, grammar, and more writing objectives such as the support the writer gives to back his or her opinion. Beyond elementary writing, students may be required to find online research on their topics to support their opinions.

Note to educators: When giving assignments that involve searching on the Internet, suggest to your students that they skip links that are designated as advertisements. Often, the word "Ad" is located prior to the clickable link.

Assignments involving non-academic as well as academic writings have endless possibilities. Students can be instructed to describe persons, places, or things. Teach them to include detailed descriptions while using a wide variety of modifiers. For example, students can be asked to write a description of a relative, a teacher, a classroom, their school, their house or apartment, their front or back yard, a park, or their family's vehicle. To incorporate grammar, require that they use at least five adjectives within their description, and have them italicize or bold them in their document, which involves teaching students to format text in the word processor. Caution: I had one of my adult English as a Second Language classes write a description of me. As I had each student read his or hers aloud, a timid young woman softly read that I was "heavy," which I no longer am, thanks to the Keto diet. The couple of ESL students in the class, who knew that being labeled "heavy" can be derogatory, laughed heartily. Though I had already taught the class that calling someone "fat" is a negative, I embraced the teachable moment to let the class know that calling someone "heavy" isn't a positive either. Since that incident, I don't recollect making that student assignment again.

Students can explain how to do things in which they are required to write their details in chronological order. For example, explaining how to get from their house or apartment to the school involves detailed descriptions given in a logical order. Have the students write how they would tell a new student to get from the classroom to the school's main office and library. Have students write how to operate something, such as how to unlock a combination lock as they may have on their gym locker at school, how to start their computer and enter a specific internet site or computer program, how to check a book out of the library, or how to ride a bicycle. Again, the topics are endless. Other writing topics could be to write a grocery list of ingredients to make one of their favorite meals or dishes and then give instructions as to how it is prepared. Writing instructions on how to make a cake or an ice cream sundae are possibilities.

Other writing assignments can involve writing poetry and song lyrics, writing a review of a movie they have viewed or of a book they have read, or writing about a concert or theater presentation they have attended. One can assign writing about favorites and least favorites, such as a favorite sport or sports team, or the least favorite food that they have eaten. Assign the writing of cards for special events or holidays. Assign the writing of a Mother's Day card. Caution: Not every child's culture celebrates Mother's Day on the same day. I learned this years ago when I had my students create a Mother's Day card on the Friday before America's traditional date for Mother's Day, the second Sunday in May. As I was printing out the cards for students who had finished writing theirs, a student told me, "Mother's Day was on Wednesday." This is when I learned that the Hispanic culture celebrates Mother's Day on May 10 every year, which is often not on the second Sunday of the month. I told the Hispanic students in the class to give their Mother's Day cards to their mothers late anyway. Since then, I have timed the project to be prior to May 10.

Another concern is the possibility of having a student who doesn't have a mother. These students can be told to create a card for another person who is close to them, such as a grandmother, aunt, or a close family friend. In fact, when creating writing assignment topics, it is often a good idea to offer students choices. I find that they like having choices or options. Therefore, when making writing assignments, I sometimes give students three topics from which to choose. Doing this diminishes the number of students who sit at their computers and hesitate to start writing. The students, who procrastinate at times, are more likely to pick one of the three options and start writing.

More than simply instructing students to write about their summer or summer vacation at the beginning of the school year, give them the option of writing about their best vacation or best summer ever. They could write about the place they want to see someday and the reasons they want to go there. Throughout the year, they could be assigned to write about the last movie or television show they viewed, the best book they ever read, or their favorite television show while telling what it is about and why they enjoy it. Writing about their best friend, their favorite relative, their pets or a pet they would like to have, their favorite teacher, and so many more topics gets them to think, to remember, and to envision their future. A Friday topic can be to write about plans for the weekend, followed by an update on Monday in which the students reveal if or how their weekend plans materialized.

These topics could become a separate file on their computer or flash drive with the entries labeled "Assigned Journal" as opposed to their "Personal Journal" writings. Have them create distinctive titles and file names for each assignment. While saving these writing topics, teach students to save and organize document files in folders on their computer and the devices on which they save their documents.

…

To create an editing assignment, I write and upload a writing that has intentional errors. The students are instructed to edit the errors without using a spell check and a grammar check. It is a worthwhile language arts activity. Whimsically, I have made intentional and obvious content errors in my writings, which the students are to correct. For example, one of my most popular writings involved a Whopper from McDonald's and a Frosty from Burger King. The students caught and changed those errors, as well as the intentional spelling, grammar, and punctuation errors in the document.

...

Sample of a "Project"

Writing with purpose is educational and can be very beneficial. One of my lessons involved students writing letters and designing a petition, which was presented to the Mayor of Joliet, Illinois, regarding a busy intersection near our school. The busiest street ran north and south without even having a yield sign, let alone a stop sign or a traffic light. The east and west street had stop signs. Many students cross the street running north and south to get to school and to return home. In spite of crossing guards being added to the location, it still had been a dangerous location for all pedestrians.

The class accumulated data as to approximately how many vehicles passed north and south on the street during the half hour before school started and the half hour after school ended during the weekdays. In addition, the number of students crossing the street on school days during those times was documented. The petition, which was made available to parents during parent-teacher conferences, included the data. We took photographs and videos of the daily traffic with cars often travelling dangerously and too fast through the intersection. Unfortunately, one photo showed a student nearly being struck by a commercial vehicle that thundered through the intersection when many students were instructed to walk across the crosswalk by a crossing guard. The intersection was incredibly dangerous.

Though I don't recall the number, many parents and teachers signed the petition. I delivered the signed petition, the photos, and the student letters to the Mayor's Office. After the project was completed, I was informed that the process had begun for the government officials to evaluate the location and to determine if the intersection warranted a traffic light. Naturally, I informed my principal of what I was doing before I presented the project to the students. After all, principals don't like surprises, as the principal who hired me at the Joliet school told me during my interview for the teaching job.

Long story short, four-way traffic lights were erected in the not-too-distant future. Besides my students seeing the positive results from organizing and writing requests to a government official, I received an award for 'excellence in teaching' for creating and administering the class project. Having students write letters with a purpose can teach good writing and good citizenship.

Unfortunately, there are naysayers even when something is done for the students' benefit. One teacher, who often saw the negatives in things, told me after the stop lights had been installed, "Have you seen how backed up the traffic is in the morning with those stop lights of yours? It's so hard to get in and out of the back parking lot now!" Obviously, backed-up traffic and inconvenience in entering and exiting the school's back parking lot are not nearly as bad as having cars speeding down the street and endangering the students who cross the intersection to get to and from school. Furthermore, a parking lot in the front of the school, which has plenty of parking spots, is located down the side street where it is easy to enter and exit the school's property. As in preparing educational activities and lessons, don't be discouraged by the naysayers. Do what is right.

I was delighted to see that this traffic light project inspired one of my eighth-grade classes to write letters and create a petition of their own. They devised a petition to present to the school principal. Their concern was that they had Physical Education class at the far southeast corner of the school building first period of the school day and then had my Computer Lab class at the far northwest corner of the building second period. Though they claimed to have a very difficult time getting from the gymnasium to my class within three minutes, I remained strict about students being on time to my class. The petition to the principal requested that passing periods be lengthened two minutes, naturally allowing students more time to get from one class to another throughout the day.

The principal's response was that she could present the request to the faculty, even though she didn't think the idea would be popular. She said that Illinois schools are required to have classes in session a certain number of minutes per day. Therefore, if minutes were added to passing periods between classes, those minutes would not be taken away from class time. Instead, those minutes would be added to the end of the school day, which meant school would dismiss for the day at approximately 3:10 instead of 2:50 every day. Hearing that explanation, my students immediately dropped the request for lengthening passing periods. Again, however, it was very pleasing to see that the students were inspired to initiate a petition for something that concerned them.

…

Additional long-term assignments can involve the writing of short stories and plays, too. Possibly incorporate grammar by instructing students to write a short story with specific guidelines, such as writing the story in the present tense and in the third person.

…

Sample-writing assignments that can be done with writing classes:

Writing a "Class Prophecy" is an assignment that I have given to my graduating students within the last couple of weeks of the school year. I took the term "prophecy" from my elementary school's graduations, as a "Class Prophecy" was written and read at the eighth-grade graduations at the elementary school I attended back in the day. In other words, this is not an original assignment idea of mine. I am passing it down through the ages. Rather than having the assignment actually done for my students' graduation, I assign the creative writing assignment for my graduating classes' consumption only. These are the instructions given to students for writing the "Class Prophecy."

"Class Prophecy Assignment"

Every Eighth-Grade student will write a "Class Prophecy." Loosely defined, a prophecy is a prediction of what will happen in the future. At times, a prophecy is distinguished from a prediction in that a prophecy sometimes has religious connotations. This assignment is not for incorporating religious connotations, however. So why not call it "Class Predictions" instead of "Class Prophecy," you may ask. The reason is simple. I'm nostalgic, and this is what my English teachers called the assignment when I was in eighth grade. Anyway, you are to write a fictional, futuristic story about what your classmates will be doing twenty years from now. It's fictional, naturally, because nobody knows for sure what any of us will be doing two decades from now.

Your assignment is to predict what everyone will be doing 20 years from now, when most of your classmates will be approximately 35 years old. Organize your thoughts in a list, which contains each classmate's name followed by what you think he or she will be doing at that time. With your notes, write a final story in paragraphs, which will be given a writing grade.

Extra credit: For extra credit, add a paragraph to the end of the "Class Prophecy" about your classmates in which you predict what your eighth-grade teachers will be doing 20 years from now.

Note: While creativity and humor are encouraged, disrespecting a person is not appropriate.

Write the class' prophecy in Microsoft Word. Title your prophecy as "My Classmates – Prophecy" and save it as (YourName/ClassPeriodNumber/Prophecy) in your English folder.

…

Sample of a "Proofreading Assignment"

Note to educators: This sample has various writing errors. Similar assignments can be created with only capitalization errors, only grammar errors, or only punctuation errors, depending on the goals and objectives set for your students' needs.

Directions: Rewrite the following paragraph without errors. There is at least one error, usually more, in each sentence. The errors may be in spelling, capitalization, grammar, punctuation, or something else. Do this assignment in Notepad.

"Proofreading Assignment"

　　A lady in our nieghborhood called the police to report a burglery. She said that a man was see entering her nieghbors house, quickly. Accordin to her statements he left the house jus as quickly. She also said that the man was carring some box when he left. Therefore she could assume that a robbry was taking place When the police ask the woman caller to discribe the thief, she gave the following discription:
　　The burglar was a white man who looked to be about 7 foot taller. He have medium-length bright red hare. He was wearing a pink hat with a flour in it that was much to small for him. He was also waring a purple shirt with big yellow and white flours pictured on it. His pants were extremley baggy and much to short for him. They had wide verticle stripes that were red white and blue. He had an white sock on one foot and none on other. Finally he had awkwerd shoes on his foot. They were orunge with big yellow shoe lace.
　　after the detailed discription the policemen ask, "Is this guy crazy or what"? The woman caller says, "No, I think he's a clown." After the phone call, the policeman gone down to the local carnivel and arrested Bozo Dobo, the clown.

Note to educators: I create proofreading assignments with the intentional errors in a word processor that does not automatically correct spelling and grammar errors by default, such as Microsoft Word does. It is easier to create without the errors automatically corrected. Additionally, I have students do the assignment in a word processor that does not automatically correct spelling and grammar, as I want them to correct the document's errors without assistance. The proofreading assignment above was created in Microsoft's My Notebook program.

…

Sample of a "Grammar Assignment"

Directions: The following paragraph is written in the present tense. In Microsoft Word (a word processing program), rewrite the paragraph in the future tense. When completed, skip a line and rewrite the paragraph in the past tense.

A sample of each tense: Present tense = I walk to school. Future tense = I will walk to school. Past tense = I walked to school

The paragraph:

      I leave my house and walk three blocks to the grocery store. At the grocery store, I go to the aisle that has snack foods. From the snack aisle, I go to different aisles to buy a loaf of wheat bread, a gallon of skim milk, a medium size jar of peanut butter, and a small jar of grape jelly. I pay the cashier and go back to my house. At my house, I turn on the television and watch one of my favorite television programs. Then I go to the kitchen and make myself a peanut butter and jelly sandwich and pour myself a big glass of milk. I eat the sandwich and drink the milk. Then my brother comes in the house and wants me to make him a sandwich and to get him a big glass of milk. Like other times, I tell him to make his own sandwich and to pour his own glass of milk.

Note to educators: If keyboarding practice is not desired, students can simply write the correct verbs for each tense, as follows:

Present tense: leave, walk, go, go, pay, go, turn, watch, go, make, pour, eat, drink, comes, wants, tell.

Past tense: left, walked, went, went, paid, went, turned, watched, went, made, poured, ate, drank, came, wanted, told.

Future tense: Will leave, will walk, will go, will go, will pay, will go, will turn, will watch, will go, will make, will pour, will eat, will drink, will come, will want, will tell.

...

Sample of "Correcting Run-On Sentences Assignment"

Directions: Type the following paragraphs. Correct the run-on sentences by putting a period (and a space) at the end of each sentence. Remember to begin each sentence with a capital letter. Reminder: a sentence is one complete thought and must have a subject and a predicate.

The paragraphs:

>we are doing this writing activity because some students are writing journals and other written assignments without proper sentences a sentence must have a capital letter at the beginning and a period or other punctuation mark at the end such as a question mark or an exclamation mark a proper sentence has a subject and a predicate the subject of the sentence tells who or what the sentence is about the predicate tells something about the subject of the sentence the subject of a sentence is usually a noun or a pronouns but can also be absent from the sentence when a subject is absent from a sentence the subject is called understood

>here is an example of a sentence with a subject being a noun our school is a junior high school here is an example of a sentence with a subject being a pronoun it is a school here is an example of a sentence with the subject being understood go to the school just remember that one complete thought is one complete sentence put a capital letter at the beginning and a period or another punctuation mark at the end

…

Another creative writing activity is to have the students create a document with intentional errors, which may be selected as a class assignment in the future. To be certain that the students are making intentional errors rather than actual errors in the assignment, have them italicize the intentional errors in the document that they type. Of course, if an error is in missing punctuation, the error cannot be formatted.

Here is how one student began his assignment:

>**on sunday, me and my friends** went out for **a wile**. We went to **a movies** and then went to a **restraunt** to eat. We went to

pizza hut where I **eat to** much. That **don't** stop me from getting **a icecream sunday** at **dairy queen** on the way home, though.

…

"Commonly Misspelled Words Assignment"

To assist students with improving their spelling abilities, they are given a list of commonly misspelled words. There are a number of misspelled spelling word lists on the Internet and in print. I have used William Strunk's "The Elements of Style" list of misspelled words, as well as words with the addition of misspellings I have commonly found in students' assignments.

The words include: accidentally; formerly; privilege; advice; humorous; pursue; affect; hypocrisy; repetition; beginning; immediately; rhyme; believe; incidentally; rhythm; benefit; latter; ridiculous; challenge; led; sacrilegious; criticize; lose; seize; deceive; marriage; separate; definite; mischief; shepherd; describe; murmur; siege; despise; necessary; similar; develop; occurred; simile; disappoint; parallel; too; duel; tragedy; ecstasy; playwright; tries; effect; preceding; undoubtedly; existence; prejudice; until; fiery; principal.

Students are given the assignments of using the words correctly in sentences. These assignments are spread out, as the word list is lengthy. In each assignment, they are allowed to use more than one of the words from the list in one sentence. After all of the misspelled words' assignments have been completed, we have an in-class spelling bee, which begins with the words they have been assigned from the misspelled words' list. Naturally, if there is no winner by the time I reach the end of the list, I have additional words to continue the activity until there is a winner. Sometime after the spelling bee activity, the class has a spelling test in which I read the words as the students write them on notebook paper. I post the name of each class winner on the board and leave it up for a day or so. I always have a small treat for each class' winner, too.

Note to the educator: If you have conducted spelling bees, you know that some students become disinterested in the spelling bee after they misspell a word and are returned to their seats. In an effort to keep the students occupied after they have been put out of the spelling bee, they are told to write the word they misspelled in the spelling bee 25 times and to write a sentence with the misspelled word included.

...

About "PowerPoint Assignments"

Microsoft PowerPoint is a presentation program consisting of a series of slides. I teach students how to make a Microsoft PowerPoint presentation, as it is a requirement for the students' annual Science Fair and their Heritage/Cultural Fair. As with other computer operations, I display a sample on the classroom's big screen and then create a basic presentation for them. Students are told that the PowerPoint's writing is to accompany a verbal presentation. Therefore, the PowerPoint's slides will most likely not have all of the content of their talk. Instead, it will only have the main ideas or a summary of what they are talking about in their presentation. Additionally, students are instructed to have slides with outlines, as it gives them (as a presenter), as well as their audience, a guide to follow.

Naturally, after learning how to operate PowerPoint, students need to be taught the following language arts skills: how to formulate main ideas and produce a summary of content, as well as how to make an outline to accompany their content.

To practice creating a PowerPoint presentation, the students are told to create an assignment called "All about Me." Each student types out his or her personal timeline, which includes the important events in his or her life from his or her birth to the present. Then each student creates a PowerPoint about their life, based on the timeline. For example, the first slide will have the title "All about Me" as well as the student's full name, the date and time of his or her birth, and the location of his or her birth. The second slide may be the student's baptism or the birth of a sibling, depending on the next major event in the student's life. Some items within their PowerPoint may be the time they started attending a particular school, the time they moved to their current house, when they took a memorable family vacation, or when a grandparent passed away. Logically, the last slide will be about the student's present day, including his or her age, location, and grade in school.

After going through the process of creating their personal PowerPoint about themselves, they should have the experience necessary to create their presentation slides for the Science Fair and Heritage/Cultural Fair, which will occur later in the school year.

Note to educators: The Microsoft PowerPoint program has tutorials and templates, which can greatly assist a teacher with introducing the program to students. The program and related language arts skills required for a successful PowerPoint presentation are challenging for some students. Therefore, pairing or grouping of students to work together, as a method of student mentoring, may be assistive.

…

Sample of a "Biography Assignment"

Students are taught about biographical writings and then instructed to write one. Though some educators may want the biography to be about a historical figure, I allow students to choose any "famous person," as I want to motivate the students to write the assignment as they embrace a personal interest.

"Biography Assignment"

Directions: Write a biography about a famous person. The person may have been a United States President, a famous scientist, an astronaut, an educator, a writer, a poet, a singer, a guitar player, a business owner, or involved with any other occupation.

On the Internet, find information about the person's private and personal life. Read the highlights of the person's life, including information that tells why he or she is famous.

As you read the information about the person, take notes. The notes will be used when writing the biography. In your notes, include the names of the webpages and the URL addresses, and include this information separately at the end of the biography. Have at least two sources listed. If a biography is about President John F. Kennedy, for example, the writer of the biography could list "John F. Kennedy" at Wikipedia.com and "John F. Kennedy – Facts, Presidency & Assassination – History" at History.com.

Your report must be written in your own words. Do not copy from the webpages or any other materials you use.

After you have written about the person, write a brief paragraph in which you tell your opinion of the person, such as telling whether you find him or her to be a positive role model in your life, or if the person motivates you. Then tell why you have such an opinion of the person.

Like any other assignment, type your name, class period, and the assignment's due date in the upper left-hand corner. The title of this assignment is the name of the person of whom you are writing.

The Biography should be completed within one week from today. Write the final copy of the Biography in Microsoft Word and save it to your English folder as: (YourName/ClassPeriodNumber/Biography)

…

Sample of "Autobiography Assignment"

Students are taught about autobiographical writings and then instructed to write their own. The assignment flows well after students have created personal timelines, a PowerPoint about their lives, and a biography earlier in the school year. This activity also involves interviewing skills, as I prompt them to interview their parents and others to gain information appropriate for their autobiographical writings.

"Autobiography Assignment"

Directions: Write an autobiography, which is your life story. Tell your story in chronological order. Begin by telling when and where you were born, who your parents are, and, if any, who your siblings are. As your story progresses, tell if your family moved to different locations and if any siblings or pets have been a part of your family. You might want to include information about grandparents or others who have been an important part of your life.

After the introductory paragraph, write about the first school you attended, as well as other schools you may have attended before you came to this school. Tell the interesting tales and memories you have of these years. Whether some memories are good times or bad times, mention the ones that have been the important times in your life.

Your next paragraph should concentrate on what is going on in your life in recent times. Include sports, music, extra-curricular activities, and group activities of which you participate outside of school, such as a youth group at church, Girl Scouts, and Boy Scouts.

The concluding paragraph should be futuristic. Tell what you want to do later in life in terms of family, schooling, occupation, and anything else you envision as becoming an important part of your future.

Share this assignment with your family members. Interview them to find out information you may not know but may want to include in your life's story.

Like any other assignment, type your name, class period, and the assignment's due date in the upper left-hand corner. The title of this assignment is your name.

The Autobiography should be completed within two weeks from today. Write the final copy of your Autobiography in Microsoft

Word and save it to your English folder as: (YourName/ClassPeriodNumber/Autobiography).

Note to educators: Delicately inform students that "family secrets" are not to be divulged. I jest that most of us have that "Uncle Arthur" or some other relative that the family never talks about in public. I conclude, "Keep Uncle Arthur out of your autobiography." Grading of the assignment is based on a student's apparent effort, completeness, and writing abilities.

…

"Year End Review Assignment"

At the end of the calendar year or at the very beginning of a new calendar year, students can integrate recent news events with writing by researching and writing about the top ten stories of the past year, in their opinion. A short paragraph about each of the news stories they choose can be written in order from the story they believe was the most impactful story of the past year to the tenth story. Perhaps students can write an additional paragraph in which they explain why they believe their top story is most impactful to society.

…

Sample of a "Description Assignment"

Note to educators: Bring an interesting-looking item to class that students likely haven't seen before, such as an old phonograph or an uncommon musical instrument. Possibly, you could simply show a picture of an item.

The students' writing assignment is to describe what they see, to suggest what it might be used for, and to give the item an original name.

After students have completed the assignment, tell them what the item is called and what it is used for, or has been used for in the past when it was well known. Then, in writing, have them create a newspaper or magazine advertisement for the item, or any item you assign.

…

Letter writing is a worthwhile lesson and activity for students. After distinguishing between a friendly letter and a business letter, assign both. Beyond the correctly formatted letters, create envelopes. On rare occasion, the students' letters are mailed, which creates excitement when letters receive written responses.

…

Email writing and email etiquette involving professional writing can be taught. However, depending on the age of the students, the exchange of emails with persons they do not know is ill advised.

…

Remind students the benefits of learning to write, which include: writing is an effective way of communicating to others; writing improves one's verbal as well as writing skills; writing can help clear one's mind and help a person put things into perspective; writing helps a person remember things he or she needs to remember; writing helps one remember thoughts and ideas that a person doesn't want to forget; writing can promote individual creativity; writing can give a feeling of having accomplished something; writing exercises one's mind; writing well improves academic performance; and, writing well can assist a person in getting a good job.

Math

Integrating math with language arts has come into being through the years. Beyond having student read word math problems to be solved, an appropriate writing assignment is to have students describe in written words about their method of solving a math problem. This totally integrates writing and math. Another similar assignment is having students create word math problems. After the teacher reviews the completed assignments for comprehension and mathematic accuracy, the mathematic word problems created by students can be distributed for the entire class to solve. Students are motivated to do their best by knowing that the teacher will assign the most creative word problems to the entire class.

...

"Stock Market Activity"

Students can study the stock market online with its multitude of learnings involving finance, business, and numbers. There are numerous stock market courses online, which teach students the vocabulary involved with the stock market, as well as teaching them the many aspects of the stock market, including the buying and selling of stocks and the tracking of profits and losses. Many of these sites, however, have a cost. Fortunately, for several years, my school's administration saw the educational advantage of teaching the stock market, and it allowed my students access to an online stock market course.

Even without an online program, however, students can imaginarily buy and sell stocks while watching the stocks' movements online. The students enter the stocks they decide to purchase and the stocks' data into a spreadsheet. Monetary values and percentages become interesting to them as they analyze their imaginary purchases rise and fall in value. During these activities, students are taught how to create formulas in spreadsheets as the tool performs their monetary calculations for them. This is a good time to have students accompany their spreadsheet with line graphs, as it gives their stock market portfolio a clear and interesting visual.

…

Sample of a unit's "Vocabulary Building"

When appropriate, develop students' vocabulary while teaching a unit. Create a list of words related to the unit being taught and have students define or use the words in writing. The following is a partial list that can be used for an "Economics and Stock Market Unit."

"Economics and Stock Market Vocabulary"

Economics are the study of how we produce and distribute our wealth.

Service is any action that one person or group does for another in exchange for payment.

Goods are any items that can be bought or sold.

Resource is anything used to produce a good or service.

Production is the process of changing the raw materials of the resource into some economic good or service that can be used to satisfy desires.

Plentiful means easy to find or more than enough of a supply of an item.

Scarce means hard to find or not enough to meet demand.

Renewable is something that can be replaced.

Nonrenewable is a resource that cannot be replaced once it is used up.

Needs are necessary for survival.

Wants are desires not necessary for survival.

Supply is the degree of availability of an item.

Demand is the usefulness of an item or how many people want to buy it.

Surplus results when the supply is greater than the demand.

Scarcity results when the demand is greater than the supply.

Consumption is the way we use produced goods.

Interdependence is the way the production and consumption of goods and services are divided among many different individuals and groups.

Interest, in finance, is the money the bank pays depositors for the privilege of borrowing their money until they need it back again.

Loan is the money given to a borrower temporarily that must be paid back fully with interest.

Depositor is a person who puts money in a bank.

Federal Reserve is the main regulator of banks in the United States.

Bond, in finance, is a certificate issued by the government or business that needs to borrow money and will pay the buyer back later with interest.

Recession is less money in the economy that causes a decline in demand.

Inflation is an increase in the amount of money in the economy.

Depression is a severe recession that results in a decline in business, high unemployment, and lowered stock market values.

Denominations are the amounts in which money is printed.

Consumer is a buyer of a good or service.

Producer is someone who makes goods or provides services.

Mint means making coins.

Bank is an institution for saving and lending.

Shares are units of equity ownership interest in a corporation that exist as a financial asset providing for an equal distribution in any residual profits.

Shareholders are the people who own shares.

Dividend is the distribution of some of a company's earnings to its shareholders.

Equity is the amount of money that would be returned to a company's shareholders if the company were to end its operations.

Stock market is the community of individuals and corporations engaged in the buying and selling of shares of companies.

Stocks are the shares of companies that investors buy and sell.

Investor is a person or organization that puts money into a financial scheme or property with the expectation of achieving a profit.

Profit is a financial gain.

Loss, in finance, is the loss of money or decrease in financial value.

Finance, as a noun, is the management of money; as a verb, finance is to provide funding or money for a person or enterprise.

Note: Educators can create solid achievement scores by testing the students' knowledge of the terms in each unit via a vocabulary quiz.

…

Have students create a timeline of mathematical discoveries or of famous mathematicians throughout history. The assignment integrates online research and writing.

Note to educators: To introduce timelines to students, create a timeline in front of them on the whiteboard or other large display. For their first hands-on experience in creating a timeline, students are assigned to create a timeline of their life, beginning with the year of their birth and ending with the current year. Then they are told to list main events in their life, which will be ordered chronologically on their timelines.

...

Sample of "Sequence of Numbers Assignment"

To understand and solve the sequencing of numbers, one has to study the numbers given, and then fill in the missing numbers.

For example, when the number sequence problem is 2, 4, 6, 8, 10 __, __, __, __, 20, the sequence is counting by twos. Therefore, the answer is 2, 4, 6, 8, 10, 12, 14, 16, 18, 20.

"Sequence of Numbers Assignment"

Directions: Do the assignment on an Excel spreadsheet. Type your name in cell A1, and type the assignment's title, SEQUENCE OF NUMBERS in cell A3.

Begin the first sequence of numbers down Column A, in cell A5 to cell A14. All columns' answers will be in rows 5 to 14. Two cells below that, in cell A16, type in the formula that will add up the cells with the numbers in that column: =SUM(A5:A14). One cell below that, in cell A17, type in the formula that will give an average of the numbers: =AVERAGE(A5:A14). Put the "sum" and "average" formulas in rows 16 and 17 for each column.

The numbers for Column A, beginning in A5, are:

-1, -2, __, __, __, __, __, __, __, -10.

The numbers for Column B, beginning in B5, are:

3, 14, __, __, __, __, __, __, __, 102.

The numbers for Column C, beginning in C5, are:

-100, -105, -95, -110, -90, __, __, __, __, -125.

The numbers for Column D, beginning in D5, are:

8000000, 4000000, __, __, __, __, __, __, __, 15625.

The numbers for Column E, beginning in E5, are:

3, 9, 27, 81, ___, ___, ___, ___, ___, 59049.

The numbers for Column F, beginning in F5, are:

3, 6, 18, 72, ___, ___, ___, ___, ___, 10886400.

The numbers for Column G, beginning in G5, are:

1, 9/10, 4/5, 7/10, ___, ___, ___, ___, ___, 1/10.

Save this spreadsheet as (YourName/ClassPeriodNumber/Sequence) in your math folder.

Note to educators: any assignment where students enter numerical data into a spreadsheet lends itself to practicing calculations by entering formulas. Regarding organizational saving of assignments: when similar assignments are assigned in the future, simply add a number after the assignment name, such as Sequence1, Sequence2, etc.)

…

Sample "Data Entry/Calculation/Formatting Spreadsheet Assignment"

Directions: Using the keypad on the keyboard, enter the following numbers down column A.

(Provide a list of 30 numbers.) Two cells below the last number, enter a formula to give the sum of all the numbers in the column, =SUM(A1:A30) and two cells further down column A, enter a formula to give the average of the numbers, =AVERAGE(A1:A30). Sort the 30 numbers in cells A1 through A30 from smallest to largest. Italicize the numbers that are at or below the average for the list of numbers. In cell C1, enter your first and last name. Save this spreadsheet as (YourName/ClassPeriodNumber/DataEntry) to your math folder.

Note to educators: Other numerical data that can be used for practicing spreadsheets and the creation of graphs and charts include the recording of the student's test and quiz scores as well as typing-speed scores.

...

Spreadsheet Project: "My Personal Expense Account Assignment"

Directions:

Using Microsoft's Excel spreadsheet program, type "My Personal Expense Account" in cell A1. Format the title to be bold, italicized, Times New Roman font, and sized 14 cpi (characters per inch).

In cell A2, type your first and last names. Format your name to be bold, Times New Roman font, and sized 14 cpi.

In cell B4, type tomorrow's date in numerical form, in bold letters, Times New Roman font, and sized 14 cpi. Type the date of the day after tomorrow in cell C4 with the same formatting, and type the date of the day after that in cell D4 with the same formatting.

In cell E4, type the word TOTALS in all capital letters, bold, italicized, Times New Roman font, and sized 14 cpi.

The Categories Column:

In cell A5, type the word FOOD in all capital letters, bold, and sized 14 cpi.

In cell A6, type the word CANDY in all capital letters, bold, and sized 14 cpi.

In cell A7, type the word ENTERTAINMENT in all capital letters, bold, and sized 14 cpi.

In cell A8, type the word TRANSPORTATION in all capital letters, bold, and sized 14 cpi.

In cell A9, type the word PERSONALS in all capital letters, bold, and sized 14 cpi.

In cell A10, type the word CLOTHES in all capital letters, bold, and sized 14 cpi.

In cell A11, type the word SCHOOL SUPPLIES in all capital letters, bold, and sized 14 cpi.

In cell A12, type the word MISCELLANEOUS in all capital letters, bold, and sized 14 cpi.

In cell A13, type the word TOTALS in all capital letters, bold, italicized, and sized 14 cpi.

Formatting the cells that have the daily and categorical totals:

In cell B13, type the following formula: =SUM(B5:B12). Don't forget the equal sign before the word SUM, the colon between the cells B5 and B12, and the parentheses around the cell names. This formula tells the spreadsheet to give the sum or total of the first day's numbers put in cells B5, B6, B7, B8, B9, B10, B11, and B12.

Copy and Paste the formula typed in cell B13 to cells C13 and D13. This will give a total amount at the bottom of three dated columns.

In cell E5, type the following formula: =SUM(B5:D5). Again, don't forget the equal sign before the word SUM, the colon between the cells B5 and D5, and the parentheses around the cell names. This formula tells the spreadsheet to give the sum or total of the FOOD amount numbers put in cells B5, C5, and D5.

Cut and Paste the formula typed in cell E5 to cells E6, E7, E8, E9, E10, E11, E12, and E13. This will give a TOTAL amount at the end of each of the category rows as well as a total of the TOTALS calculated in B13, C13, and D13.

Format for currency:

Highlight from cell B5 to E13 with the mouse or the keyboard's shift key and arrow keys, and click on the $ (dollar sign) button in the Number section at the top of the spreadsheet. This will show all of your amounts in these cells in the spreadsheet as currency (with a dollar sign and a two-place decimal). Tomorrow and the next two days, enter the amount of money you spend in each of these categories. Incidentally, if you spend money that doesn't fit into one of the seven categories, put that amount in the MISCELLANEOUS category. Miscellaneous means of various types or from different sources.

Keep track of the money you spend tomorrow and the next two days so you will have an accurate spreadsheet account of your expenses.

Save the assignment as (YourName/ClassPeriodNumber/Expenses) to your math folder. As always, click on cell A1 to make it active before saving the file so that your file will open up on top.

Note to educators: When the expense account spreadsheet is completed, teach graph and chart making. The totals in the spreadsheet can be turned into various types of charts on the computer, such as line, bar, and pie graphs and charts.

…

Follow-up activity: "Continuing My Personal Expense Account Assignment"

After the "My Personal Expense Account Assignment" is completed, the data can be manipulated beyond what has already been performed by the students.

Continuing My Personal Expense Account

Instructions: In the spreadsheet program, open your "My Personal Expense Account" spreadsheet and do the following:

Type "Daily Average" in cell F4, "Weekly Projection" in cell G4, "Monthly Projection" in H4, "Yearly Projection" in I4 (the letter I and the number 4).

Create a formula to find the "daily average" of each category's expenses in column F, (cells F5 through F12).

Create a formula to find the "weekly projection" of each category's expenses in column G, (cells G5 through G12).

Create a formula to find the "monthly projection" of each category's expenses in column H, (cells H5 through H12).

Create a formula to find the "yearly projection" of each category's expenses in column I, (cells I5 through I12).

To figure the "daily average" and "projections," remember the following: To figure the daily average, the total expenses for all of the days is divided by the number of days in the spreadsheet, (three days). With the daily average, figure the weekly projection by remembering that there are 7 days in a week. With the daily average, figure the monthly projection by considering there are 30 days in a month (though some months have 31 days and February has 28, or 29 in a Leap Year). With the daily average, figure the yearly projection by considering there are 365 days in a year (though every year that is a multiple of four is a Leap Year and has 366 days.)

Format the new entries on the spreadsheet as the other entries have been formatted, which includes all monetary amounts being formatted as currency.

Save the revised spreadsheet assignment as (YourName/ClassPeriodNumber/Expenses2) to your math folder.

When all of the above calculations have been inserted into your Personal Expense Account's spreadsheet, do the following to create a "Bar Graph":

"Cut and paste" the category titles beneath the active cells down column A; type the categories' totals in column B; then create a "Bar Graph" and save it with the spreadsheet saved as "Expense2."

Educators: Spreadsheet formula activities can be challenging for some students. The pairing of students for mentoring purposes is advised.

…

"Career Assignment"

Note to educators: This assignment is loosely placed in the Mathematics unit because of the impact that many occupations have on the economy as well as on one's personal income.

Directions: Using the Internet to find information and Microsoft Word to write a report, write about a career. It is best for you to choose a career you may want to enter in the future, so that you can learn more about the career as you do this assignment. On the Internet, read information about the career or job at two or more websites. While taking notes, write down the name of the webpages and/or URL addresses, and include this information separately at the end of the report. For example, write: "How to Become a Television Announcer: Career Roadmap" at Study.com and "Announcer" at Wikipedia.com.

Write a report about the career, including such information as what a person does on the job, the education suggested or required for acquiring the job, the salary range, and current or future job availabilities. Additionally, the report could include the positive and negative aspects of working in the career.

The last paragraph of your report should tell why you chose this career for your report topic as well as why this career is possibly the job you want to have in the future.

Your report must be written in your own words. Do not copy from the webpages you find.

The Career assignment should be completed within one week from today. Write the final copy of the Career report in Microsoft Word and save it to your Math folder as: (YourName/ClassPeriodNumber/Career)

...

The "Resume Assignment"

A logical assignment to follow the "My Personal Expense Account" and "Career Assignment" is the writing of a resume. While some students may be rather young for needing a resume, it is a skill worth teaching, as all students will have use for a resume in a few short years. I provide the following written document in explanation, and create a fictional resume that is displayed before them. After the explanation and demonstration, the students are given the assignment of writing a resume. The document provided to the students follows:

"Personal Resume Assignment"

A resume is a written document that a person creates in order to obtain employment. It should tell a prospective employer information that a job-seeker believes would assist him or her in being hired for a job.

A resume should include the following:

A "heading," which is created by centering your full name, address, telephone number, and email address at the top of the document. (Format your name as 14 cpi and the rest of the document at 12 cpi; use the Times New Roman font for the entire document).

An "objective," which is placed two lines below the heading and left aligned. Write the objective as a statement that briefly states what you want to accomplish from preparing the resume. Objectives start with the word "To" and are followed by a verb, then a noun, and then another phrase, such as: "To obtain summer employment as a newspaper delivery person." (Sometimes this section is replaced by one's "professional summary.")

Your "education" needs to be listed chronologically. Include the names of the schools you have attended, their locations, and the years you attended the schools.

Your "work experiences" should be listed, if you have any former work experiences. Like your education, list the work experiences chronologically, giving names of the business or the person for whom you worked, as well as the addresses where and dates when you worked. (Sometimes this section is called one's "work history.")

Your "skills" can be included. This is where you list any specific skills you have that may be useful on the job of which you are applying.

Your "hobbies and interests" should be listed to tell a potential employer additional information about yourself. This may also assist the hiring person in deciding if you are the right person for the job.

Your "community service" should be included, if you have done any community service, such as helping at a library, a school, or a church.

"Additional information" is a section of the resume in which you can add anything else you want a prospective employer to know about you that has not been mentioned already. This could include information about having made the honor roll at school or being elected to student government. If you have volunteered to help relatives or friends with projects or their businesses, this is the place to add those experiences. Stipulations regarding your offer to work can also be added in this section, such as telling the employer that you are looking for part-time employment during the summer only.

The last line of your resume could state "References available upon request." This means that you are telling the prospective employer that you are willing to give names and contact information of persons who will recommend you for the job you are seeking. A personal reference could be a former employer, a teacher, the leader of your church, or anyone else who can give an honest, informed, and positive opinion of you. Some employers do not allow family members to give a reference. Later in life, you will find that listing references is customary when applying for a job.

Note: Do not write a resume in paragraphs. Every section after the "Objective" should be written as lists or phrases.

Following is an actual resume created by a student, though her personal information has been changed for privacy's sake.

Janelle Smith

112 Ohio Street

Joliet, Illinois 60432

(815) 555-5555

Objective: To obtain summer employment.

Education: Park School in Joliet, Illinois, 2006-2007; Eisenhower Academy School in Joliet, Illinois, 2007-2010; Gompers Junior High School in Joliet, Illinois, 2010-2013.

Work Experience: Babysitting in the summers of 2011 and 2012.

Skills: Type 40 words per minute and have knowledge of Microsoft WORD and EXCEL.

Hobbies and Interests: Skating, reading, listening to music, and babysitting newborn babies.

Community Service: Feeding the homeless at Morning Star Mission with other members of my church.

Additional Information: Honor Roll student at Eisenhower and Gompers. Student Council member. Learning Spanish. I am seeking full-time employment for the summer and part-time weekend employment in the fall.

References available upon request.

…

If Compton's Britannica or a similar resource is available to a school online, students could read economy-related (and other academic area) articles. Create assignments in which students find information and possibly answer high-order thinking skill questions. Naturally, even without a subscriptions to educational sites, there are free websites that offer similar information.

Sample of a "Compton's Britannica Encyclopedia Assignment"

"Economy Reference Search Assignment"

1. Define "economics,' as defined within the first section of the "Economics" article in the Compton's Britannica Encyclopedia.

2. The word "economy" originally referred to household management – from the _____ oikos meaning "household," and nomos meaning "rule," or "governance."

3. When was economics originated?

4. Within the same article, find microeconomics. What are they?

5. Within the same article, find macroeconomics. What are they?

Use the "Money" article for the next three questions:

6. In the "Money" article, you will find what barter means. What does it mean?

7. What two things are called hard money?

8. When was the first hard money used?

…

Sample of student-created "Math Word Problems"

Directions: Create math word problems, sometimes referred to as story problems, in which addition, subtraction, multiplication, and division are used to solve the problems.

Here is a sample of one student's original word problems:

1. There were 1031 boxes and each weighed six pounds. How many pounds did all of the boxes weigh?

2. There was a large truck holding 300 pounds of boxes. There were 60 boxes of equal weight on the truck. How much did each box weigh?

3. Seven classrooms collected equal numbers of canned foods for a canned food drive. Since the total number of cans collected was 161, how many cans did each of the seven classes collect?

4. There are seven computer classes. Two of the classes have 32 students, two have 31 students, two have 29 students and one has 36. To the nearest whole number, what is the average number of students in all seven of the computer classes?

5, 6. The Chicago Bears scored seven points in the first quarter, scored twice as many points in the second quarter as they did in the first quarter, scored three times as many points in the third quarter as they did in the first quarter and scored no points in the fourth quarter. How many points did they score during the game? Additionally, the opposing team scored 18 points less than half the Bears' final score. How many points did the opposing team have?

7, 8. There are eight buses, each bus has 33 seats, and two people can sit in each seat. Therefore, what is the total number of people that can sit on all eight of the buses? Additionally, if five of the buses are full, two buses are two-thirds full, and one bus is half-full, how many people are on the eight buses, including a bus driver on each bus?

9. Henry had $14.15 in the morning when he went to school. His friend Robert gave him $2.50 that he owed him from yesterday. Another friend, Jessica, borrowed one-tenth of the amount Robert gave Henry. At school, Henry spent $1.00 for a flash drive, $1.25 for other school supplies, as well as paying $5.00 that had to be paid in order to go on next week's field trip. Then he spent $1.40 for his school lunch. After school, he spent $2.00 plus 8% tax on snacks. How much money did Henry have left?

10. Jack has 12 bags of candy, and each bag has 12 pieces of candy. If he gives an equal amount to each one of his 27 classmates and teacher, how many pieces does he have left?

...

Remind students the benefits of learning mathematics, which include: math is a portion of most careers in one way or another; math helps a person with his or her finances; math improves problem-solving skills; math is universal and helps people understand one another; knowing math can help a person shop economically; math comes in to play in everyday activities such as using a phone and other devices, setting time schedules, paying for expenses, and even cooking; and, learning math not only makes one more intelligent but makes a person appear more intelligent to others.

Science

Science and medicine can go hand in hand, and they are especially pertinent and hold interest since science has been in the headlines since the Covid-19 outbreak in early 2020. The current events involving science and medicine make appropriate reading and research assignments. The medicines, tests, health issues, vaccines, and more can be research topics, which involve reading comprehension and writing assignments for students.

Through written materials and videos, the Internet has information on such science topics as the human body and the digestive system, animals and insects, plants and trees, the solar system and space travel, the weather and the seasons, water and natural resources, Earth and the stars, sources of energy and machines, and a great deal more. A display of the many science-related topics that are researchable on the Internet assists students with finding topics that may interest them and may serve them well in their search for science fair topics, as well.

Integrate history with science by assigning readings and writings about the important scientists.

Create and administer tests about the science readings that have been assigned to check the students' completion and comprehension of the assignments.

Have students create timelines of science events or of scientists and their accomplishments throughout history. The assignment will involve the integration of online research and writing.

…

Activities accompanying "The Greatest Paper Airplane" Unit

After visiting websites regarding the popular science topic of making paper airplanes, students make paper airplanes while reading the history of flight. A test created to accompany "The Greatest Paper Airplane" unit follows.

"The Greatest Paper Airplane Test"

Directions: Write the answer to each question in complete sentences.

1. Who believed that we could learn how to fly by imitating birds?

2. Where did the Wright brothers make the world's first powered airplane flight?

3, 4. How long and how fast was the flight?

5. What is the study of forces that affect an object moving through air?

6. What is the constant force that pulls the plane toward the ground?

7. What is the force that comes from an airplane's engine?

8, 9, 10, 11. What are the four movable surfaces that a pilot controls during flight?

Answer Key: 1. Leonardo da Vinci; 2. Kitty Hawk, North Carolina; 3-4. 120 feet and 35 miles per hour; 5. aerodynamics; 6. gravity; 7. thrust; 8-11. aileron, flap, elevator, and rudder.

...

As explained in the "English: Reading" section of this book, have students create a crossword puzzle about the science units and the scientists being studied, such as Earth including geology, weather, and ecology, as well as, space science, life science, physical science, biology, and contemporary science issues.

...

Create a word search with science terms related to a science lesson. Once again, there are many websites where word searches can be created, including WordMint.com.

...

If Compton's Britannica or a similar resource is available to a school online, students could read science (and other academic area) articles. Create assignments in which students find information and possibly answer high-order thinking skill questions.

…

Integrate with the computer class students' science teachers by staying informed about the units being studied in science class. Beyond supporting the science lessons with potential reading materials on the Internet, create word lists that have terms related to the science unit. Have students create an ongoing Science Dictionary.

…

Remind the students the benefits of learning science, which include: science makes a person aware of the world around him or her; science is used in vital occupations such as medicine, inventing, and engineering; knowing science helps one develop life skills; knowing science can give a person knowledge to get a good job; knowing science helps one understand health, including one's own health; knowing science helps a person make well-informed decisions throughout life.

Health

Health, sometimes incorporated into schools' science and physical education curriculum, is an objective that is appropriate and relatively simple to integrate into education on computers due to the vast amount of websites offering informative articles and videos.

As with science, since the Covid-19 pandemic became global news in early 2020, the topics of health and medicine lend themselves to health instruction.

Assign the reading of articles or the viewing of videos covering the topics to be learned. As students mature, they become more interested in their being and often want to know what will benefit them in terms of becoming a healthier person. To integrate health into education via technology, assign readings and viewings of information about the benefits of proper nutrition, as well as information on diseases, physical fitness, sexuality, and first aid.

February is National Children's Dental Health month, making February a good time to assign reading and writing assignments regarding the importance of practicing good oral hygiene to avoid problems with one's teeth and gums. A huge amount of information on dentistry and advised oral hygiene practices are available on the Internet.

Mental health is a vast topic that can be researched to incorporate reading and writing into health lessons. Online, there are lessons categorized as identifying and talking about one's feelings, understanding how feelings affect one's behaviors, methods of managing one's feelings, the connection between mental and physical health, as well as managing the transition from one stage of life to another stage, which is very relatable to students. Furthermore, there are lessons on conquering the stigma related to mental health, promoting emotional wellbeing, avoiding negative thinking, avoiding unhealthy coping strategies like self-harm and eating disorders, as well as dealing with anxiety and depression.

Students can also study the careers that are involved in the healthcare profession. Beyond doctors in many medical areas and nurses, there are physicians' and nurses' assistants, pharmacists, dentists, dental assistants, dieticians, veterinarians, lab technicians, surgeons and anesthesiologists, as well as physical, occupational, and other types of therapists.

Beyond the practicing of reading for comprehension and the practicing of listening skills, incorporate writing assignments that enhance the information the students are learning.

...

As explained in the "English: Reading" section of this book, have students create a crossword puzzle about the health units being studied, such as nutrition, vitamins, physical fitness, good habits, anti-drug abuse, anti-alcoholism, personal hygiene, cardiovascular system, etc.

...

Create a word search with vocabulary or other words related to health lessons. Once again, there are many websites where word searches can be created, including WordMint.com.

...

If Compton's Britannica or a similar resource is available to a school online, students could read health-related (and other academic area) articles. Create assignments in which students find information and possibly answer high-order thinking skill questions.

...

Integrate with the computer class students' health teachers by staying informed about the units being studied in health class. Beyond supporting the health lessons with potential reading materials on the Internet, create word lists that have terms related to the health unit. Have students create an ongoing Health Dictionary.

…

Remind the students the benefits of learning health, which include: learning about health teaches one how to prevent illness; learning about health teaches how one can promote good health or how one might damage his or her health; learning about health introduces a person to the human body; learning about health makes a person more aware of his or her overall physical, medical, and mental health; studying health may motivate students to enter a worthwhile healthcare profession, including doctors, nurses, psychologists, counselors, and physical therapists.

History and Current Events

Reading, researching, and writing assignments can integrate into online history, a branch of social studies.

Note to educators: History and Social Studies are being combined here for brevity, even though they are not interchangeable. While History is defined as the study of the various events that took place in the past and is one of the social sciences, Social Studies actually refers to the studies made with the intent of promoting social competence in which a person is to understand his or her responsibility to his or her society.

...

Historical lessons can logically start with a timeline of important dates and holidays listed chronologically from the first day of January through the last day of December. Be sure to have students incorporate all special days and holidays as not to exclude any race, nationality, religion, or gender.

Assign the reading of historical events, most appropriately assigned on or close to the historical day of the event. For example, a study of the Presidents of the United States is appropriate in February as a lead-up to Presidents' Day, which is celebrated on the third Monday in February.

...

As explained in the "English: Reading" section of this book, have students create a crossword puzzle about the history and historical figures and locations being studied, such as in American history, World history, U.S. Presidents, World War I, World War II, and other wars. Again, WordMint.com is one of the websites that can be used to create crosswords.

...

Create a word search with the events, people, vocabulary or other words that are related to a history or social studies unit. Once again, there are many websites where word searches can be created, including WordMint.com.

…

Sample of History Lesson: "Chicago, Illinois 1865 to 1889 Activity"

Note to educators: A login is needed to access the website within the Chicago Public Library website referenced in this activity. However, there are other options, including Google searches, for finding the answers to all of these questions.

Directions: Open the following website: http://www.chipublib.org/004chicago/chihist.html.

Click on the various links within this website to find the answers to the following questions. If necessary, use the "back" button to return to the main page of the website to continue the assignment. Logically, you need to consider which section of the website has the information needed to answer a question before clicking on a link.

Note to educators: If needed, you could provide the link within the website that is necessary to find the answers).

The Questions:

1. When did the Union Stock Yard open? (Use the 1865 link to answer the question.)

2. How was Lake Michigan water delivered to early Chicagoans? (Use the 1867 link to answer this question.)

3. Who was the architect of the famous Water Tower in Chicago? (Use the 1867 link to answer this question.)

4. How much did the Washington Street traffic tunnel and the second tunnel under LaSalle Street cost? Combine the two amounts to get the answer. (Use the appropriate 1869 link to answer this question.)

5. Where did the Great Chicago Fire begin? (Give the address.) (Use the 1871 link to answer this question.)

6. What was the actual date of the Great Chicago Fire? (Use the 1871 link to answer this question.)

7. Where was Chicago's first mail-order house, Montgomery Ward's, located? (Use the 1872 link to answer this question.)

8. What is the name of Chicago's first skyscraper? (Use the appropriate 1885 link to answer this question.)

9. Where is the Haymarket Riot statue presently located? (Use the 1886 link to answer this question.)

10. Who opened the historic Hull House in 1889? (Use the 1889 link to answer this question.)

Answer key: 1. 1865; 2. carried home in buckets; 3. William Warren Boyington; 4. $517,000 for the Washington Street tunnel and $566,000 for the LaSalle Street tunnel equals a total of $1,083,000; 5. in or around a barn on Patrick and Catherine O'Leary's property in the Southwest Side of Chicago at 138 DeKoven Street; 6. October 8-10, 1871; 7. at Clark and Kinzie Streets in Chicago; 8. The Home Insurance Building; 9. at the Chicago Police Headquarter located at 3510 South State Street in Chicago; 10. Jane Addams and Ellen Gates Starr.

Note to educators: To simplify the entering of a website's lengthy URL, you can provide a link on which the students may click within a word processor's document, which you can provide through the network to be accessible on all networked computers. Additionally, choosing locations for history lessons, which are in relatively close proximity to the students' location, increases interest. I have developed many lessons about Chicago and Illinois history. The schools where I have taught are close to Chicago, a location where the students have visited many times via field trips.

...

The following activities are samples of the holiday activities I assign at the appropriate times of year, which involve students reading for information and comprehension. The responses can be written on the paper or, if desired, keyed into a document.

Sample of a "Holiday Assignment"

"Memorial Day"

Directions: Search for information about Memorial Day. Answer the following questions. After your response, write the name of the webpage in which you found the answer.

1. Who first mentioned, at a social gathering in Waterloo, New York, that honor should be shown to the patriotic dead of the Civil War by decorating their graves?

2. Who was the Seneca County Clerk who helped get the holiday started by doing something with the idea?

3. What was the date of the first parade (or procession) for Memorial Day?

4. Who was the first commander of the Grand Army of the Republic who was the first person to officially recognize Memorial Day?

5. Before the holiday became known as Memorial Day, what was it called?

6. What city did the United States Government recognize as the "Birthplace of Memorial Day"?

7. Though recently celebrated on the last Monday of May, what is the official date of Memorial Day each year?

Note to administrator of this assignment: Depending on the ability levels of students, possibly assist them by suggesting that they do a Google search for "History of Memorial Day." Again, depending on the ability levels of students, possibly give the web sites where the answers to these questions can be found. For example, to find the answers to these questions, students could be guided to Britannica.com's article about Memorial Day, which is https:www.britannica.com/topic/Memorial-Day.

Answer Key: 1. Henry C. Welles; 2. John B. Murray; 3. May 5, 1966; 4. Gen. John A. Logan; 5. Decoration Day; 6. Waterloo, New York; 7. May 30.

...

To incorporate spreadsheet usage with history, have students enter the names of the United States Presidents. They enter their last names down column A; then, in column B, they enter their first names (and possibly their middle names or initials) after their last names listed in column A; then, in subsequent columns, they enter data about the years they were in office, their political parties, the dates of their birth and death, etc. To practice sorting of data, the students can sort the information they have entered into the spreadsheet alphabetically by last name, as well as by the dates in which the Presidents were in office.

...

If Compton's Britannica or a similar resource is available to a school online, students could read history-related (and other academic area) articles. Create assignments in which students find information and possibly answer high-order thinking skill questions.

...

Integrate with the computer class students' history teachers by staying informed about the units being studied in history class. Beyond supporting the history lessons with potential reading materials on the Internet, create word lists that have terms related to the history unit. Have students create an ongoing History Dictionary.

...

Remind students the benefits of learning history, which include: history teaches us about the past, and therefore we can avoid repeating past mistakes; history can give an understanding of past actions throughout the world; history shows where some of today's technology originated; history can be interesting and entertaining by learning how people lived in the past; history can make you feel good when you see how far we have come; history can teach cultural empathy; history teaches that, at the most basic level, people haven't changed; history gives an appreciation for the present.

*****

Current Events

Assigning students to read about or to watch broadcasts of current news is a beneficial lesson for appropriately aged students. The logical response to a student who claims they are not interested in the news is to assert, "You will never know how interested you are in the world until you learn what is going on in it." Or as Mother used to say about a new dish, "Try it! You might like it!"

Having students read newspapers online enhances interest in reading as well as vocabulary and comprehension. Be cautiously selective in the news stories assigned for specific student populations while being mindful of their ages. Choose stories of which they will likely find interest. Local news stories, naturally, may be a good choice, as students may relate to the locations and persons involved with the news stories. Also, news about entertainers, including famous persons in music, movies, and television, is likely something of which students will find interesting. Depending on the students, reading assignments involving sports and athletes may hit the mark in motivating them to read.

...

Assign journal writing on current event topics to encourage students to become engaged in the event as well as to allow them to express their opinions. With the Internet's inclusion of local news items, also choose reading and writing selections that will inform them and garner interest in local occurrences, issues, and politics.

...

Assign research on topics that will increase the students' knowledge and interest of their own community. These activities can integrate with history and geography, as well as language arts due to the researching, notetaking, and the ultimate writing of a report.

For example, teaching in Joliet, Illinois, assignments can be made for students to research the history of the city of Joliet and the city's County of Will, the city's and county's governmental structures, the current and past mayors, as well as the city's other historical figures including its namesake, Louis Joliet. Additionally, the city's geography, which includes the Des Plaines River, the I-55 and I-80 interstate roadways, and the city's downtown area and its neighborhoods, can be studied. Finally, the purpose and history of some of the most prominent buildings can be researched, such as the Joliet Public Library, the Will County Courthouse, the Will County Jail, Stateville Correctional Center and the Old Joliet Prison, and the city's well-known schools, which are Joliet Junior College and the University of St. Francis.

…

Have students do research for the purpose of making a list of famous people who have lived in the city where they live. Of course, if the students live in a remote area, the assignment needs to be altered to include an expanded area. Again, using Joliet, Illinois, as an example, my students can create an impressive list of entertainers including Lionel Richie, and sports figures including Gordie Gillespie. Have students choose a person from the list of famous people and write a report about the person.

Note to educators: Contact a famous person from your city to see if he or she is willing to speak to the students. A social studies teacher who worked with me knew Lionel Richie and his parents. Lionel spent part of his childhood in Joliet. Years after he graduated from Joliet East High School and became famous, he presented an informational and inspiring teleconference with our students.

…

Remind the students the benefits of learning current events, which include: current events integrates to all academic subjects; studying current events develops lifelong readers who are informed people; reading current events improves reading comprehension and vocabulary; listening to current events improves listening skills, vocabulary, and comprehension; current events teaches a person the importance of people, places, and events in the news; reading current events creates media literacy by displaying well-written models of contemporary writing; knowledge of current events gives a person many opportunities to write informed and opinionated writings; knowing current events benefits a person's interactions with others and benefits his or her conversations.

Geography

Google Maps on the Internet is a treasure chest of lessons and knowledge for teachers. With a map of Chicago's Loop on the Internet, I taught my students the reasoning behind the numbering the streets in Chicago and other cities, a skill that will become beneficial in their future when navigating around cities throughout the world. Knowing the differences between addresses that read 100 north, 100 south, 100 east, and 100 west are a relevant and valuable lesson. Make assignments involving map symbols and keys to teach students how to read map legends. Incorporate assignments that involve distances from one location to another to teach distance in mileage lessons. Naturally, this integrates with math due to the numbers involved.

With the photograph abilities in Google Maps, students not only can find a map's various locations, they can actually see the places, too. Integrate math by creating assignments solving the distance from Point A to Point B to wherever, and then returning to Point A. Furthermore, designate various miles-per-hour for different segments of the trip for students to solve how long the journey will take. The huge number of lessons can be created by using online maps.

...

Google Maps Activity

Directions: Using the Google Maps website, find directions from your house to Wrigley Field where the Chicago Cubs baseball team plays. In Google Maps, click on the 'directions' icon and have it set for travel by car. Then type your home address (including the street address, city, and state) in the "Choose starting point…" box in the upper right-hand corner of the webpage. In the "Choose your destination…" box below the starting point, type Wrigley Field's location, which is 1060 West Addison Street in Chicago, Illinois.

Answer the following questions about the information Google Maps produces:

1. How far is the shortest route from your house to Wrigley Field?

2. How long does it take to travel the quickest route from your house to Wrigley Field?

3. How many options does Google Maps give for the trip?

4. Does the quickest route include traveling on toll roads, which involves paying to travel on the roads?

Next, change your mode of transportation from traveling by car to traveling by bicycle.

5. How far is the shortest route from your house to Wrigley Field by bicycle?

6. How long does it take to travel the shortest route from your house to Wrigley Field by bicycle?

Next, change your mode of transportation from traveling by bicycle to traveling by foot or walking.

7. How far is the shortest route from your house to Wrigley Field by foot?

8. How long does it take to walk the quickest route from your house to Wrigley Field?

Notes to educators: This is a relatable assignment before taking a field trip, as the students can be given the assignment to find data regarding a trip from the school to the destination. I have used it before traveling to the Illinois State Capitol in Springfield. I have also used it before walking students to a nature center located approximately a mile from school.

...

Sample of a "City Assignment"

Directions: Using the Internet to find information and Microsoft Word to write a report, write about a city you want to visit in the future. On the Internet, read information about the place and take notes. While taking notes, write down the names of the webpages and/or URL addresses, and include this information separately at the end of the report. For example, write: "London" at Wikipedia.com, and "Welcome to London" at VisitLondon.com.

Write a report about the city, including such information as its location, population, important history, important dates, buildings, famous citizens of the present and past, and events.

The last paragraph of your report should explain why you chose this city as a place you want to visit.

Your report must be written in your own words. Do not copy from the webpages you find.

The City assignment should be completed within one week from today. Write the final copy of the report in Microsoft Word and save it to your Geography folder as:
(YourName/ClassPeriodNumber/City)

…

"Geography + Spreadsheet Activity"

To incorporate spreadsheet usage with geography, have students enter the states in the United States down column A of the spreadsheet; then, in column B, they enter the capital of each state after the state they have listed in column A; then, in subsequent columns, they enter data about the states, such as the square mile area of each state and their abbreviations as used by the U.S. Postal Service. To practice the sorting of data, have students sort the information they have entered into the spreadsheet alphabetically by state. Of course, they could also sort by other data, such as the states' areas from largest to smallest, etc.

…

If Compton's Britannica or a similar resource is available to a school online, students could read geography-related (and other academic area) articles. Create assignments in which students find information and possibly answer high-order thinking skill questions.

...

Integrate with the computer class students' geography teachers by staying informed about the units being studied in geography class. Beyond supporting the geography lessons with potential reading materials on the Internet, create word lists that have terms related to the geography unit. Have students create an ongoing Geography Dictionary.

...

Remind students the benefits of learning geography, which include: geography shows a person where they fit in our nation and within the world; geography creates a an awareness of place; geography gives a person a holistic understanding of the planet and universe; geography helps a person better understand planetary issues including climate change and global warming; geography gives a person an understanding of global issues such as energy and water concerns; and, by knowing geography, a person can become a better, more informed citizen.

Foreign Language

Learning a foreign language is not only common in education throughout the United States and beyond, it is often a student's academic requirement to graduate. According to the American Language Association, the top foreign languages studied in America's institutions of higher learning are: Spanish (which 50.2% of the foreign language students study), followed by French, American Sign Language, German, Japanese, Italian, Chinese, Arabic, Latin, Russian, Korean, Ancient Greek, Portuguese, Biblical Hebrew, and Modern Hebrew.

Due to the schools in which I have taught English and English as a Second Language in the Chicago area, my experiences with foreign language learners have involved mostly Spanish speakers. Having taught via immersion as well as via dual language, both methods of teaching English as well as Spanish can be conducted efficiently via technology. Assistive technology in learning foreign languages, as in teaching English, can be found online or on programs that are available for public use.

Incidentally, recent studies have asserted that learning a foreign language by dual and bilingual methods is better than immersion. Comparing students' first language to English is how I have taught my students since I first taught English to English as a Second Language learners in 1999, and have thereby written the book "English and Spanish: The Similarities and Differences." Again, I am a huge supporter of dual and bilingual language learning over immersion and always have been. I taught in a school that insisted on immersion for a time and found it to be less effective, if not detrimental, to the students. Additionally, I have become fluent in Spanish by learning my second language bilingually. From an educator's and a learner's perspective, I know that learning a foreign language via dual and bilingual methods works.

In fact, research in recent years has shown that dual language learning is much more effective in teaching the English and Spanish languages than using the one-language immersion method. Schools that now use dual language as opposed to language immersion are backed by research by claiming the following benefits to using two languages rather than one in learning a new language and more. The research claims that dual language learning takes advantage of the learner's capacity to learn language more quickly. These learners or students have better mental flexibility, better conceptualization, better executive functioning skills and more diversified mental abilities. Learning to read and write uses the same basic processes including phonemic awareness, decoding, fluency, comprehension, and writing mechanics. Additionally, these language learners perform as well as and often better than others on standardized tests given in English. Knowing the basic similarities between the two languages not only saves the learner time but also alleviates the guess work involved in speculating since learners can transfer their knowledge of their first language literacy to their second language. These students are said to be more aware of as well as show more positive attitudes toward other persons' cultures and are more appreciative of other people. Finally, the students are better prepared for working in a global community and are more desirable in the job market.

Thereby, many schools, if not most, are transitioning from the antiquated and less effective method of teaching languages via single-language immersion and are teaching lessons by using bilingual methods, which incorporate the comparisons of the two languages. When possible, as in English and Spanish, the comparisons of two languages makes the similarities and complicated differences easy to understand.

...

Foreign Language Assistance: Adding a Language to a Word Processor

When teaching foreign languages, it is assistive to change or add a language to the word processor. There are various ways to accomplish this. To accomplish this in Microsoft Word 10, for example, close any running applications first. Then go to the computer's 'Settings'; click on 'Time & Language'; click on 'Language'; under the "Preferred languages" section, click on the 'Add a preferred language' button; type in the name of the language desired or scroll down the list to find the language wanted. After finding the language wanted, install the language pack.

When I completed the process, I searched for Spanish since I was primarily teaching English to Spanish-speaking students who came from Mexico. After finding many options for Spanish listed by countries, I selected "Spanish (United States)" and downloaded the language pack onto the computers.

Apps and websites will appear in the first language in the list they support. By design or default, your first language is most likely 'English (United States)'.

Additionally, languages can be added by opening Microsoft Word; click on the 'Review' tab, click on 'Thesaurus' to bring up the 'Word Options' tools; under 'Set the Office Language Preferences', find 'Choose Editing Languages' where adding languages to edit documents is possible. The editing features include dictionaries, grammar checking, and sorting.

…

Foreign Language Assistance: Adding a Language to an Internet Browser

Similar to adding a language via the instructions above, a language can be added to an internet browser. To add a language to Chrome, go to the browser's 'Settings'; scroll down to the bottom of the page and click on 'Advanced'; as in the instructions above, there are options for adding languages. Additionally, you can add features such as allowing translations from other languages and allowing spell checks in the languages included in your browser.

Other methods can be used to add languages to word processors and internet browsers.

…

Writing text in Spanish

In my teaching situation, I teach my students how to write accented letters and special characters needed for writing Spanish via cryptic codes. I prefer doing this rather than changing the keyboards on the computers. After all, most computers the students encounter will not have altered keyboards, and they will need to know how to enter the accented letters from an English language-writing keyboard. Furthermore, knowing how to type accented letters is important, as some students even have accented letters in their names.

The following instructions are the method I teach students for writing the accented letters and special characters necessary to write Spanish words in Microsoft Word's word processor. Though I teach the 'Alt Key Method', there are other methods of accomplishing this keyboarding goal. The other methods are the 'Ctrl Key Method' and a method involving the 'Ctrl + Alt + Up Arrow'.

Additionally, other methods are available for writing in some other languages.

…

"Typing Accented Letters and Special Characters" via the 'Alt Key Method' for Microsoft Word

Instructions: Make sure that the 'Num Lock' key is turned on. A light may appear on your keyboard when the 'Num Lock' key is engaged. When typing the numbers in the following list, the numbers should be typed on the keypad located to the right of the keyboard's letters. Before typing the numbers, press and hold the 'Alt' key located on the lower right section of the keyboard. After typing the numbers, take your finger off the 'Alt' key. Your accented letter or special character will appear in your document. (Note: Only type the numbers. Do not type the plus sign.)

Letters for Writing in Spanish: Letras para Español

á = Alt + 0225

Á = Alt + 0193

é = Alt + 0233

É = Alt + 0201

í = Alt + 0237

Í = Alt + 0205

ó = Alt + 0243

Ó = Alt + 0211

ú = Alt + 0250

Ú = Alt + 0218

ñ = Alt + 0241

Ñ = Alt + 0209

ü = Alt + 0252

Ü = Alt + 0220

Special Characters and Punctuation Marks

¡ = Alt + 0161

¿ = Alt + 0191

« = Alt + 0171

» = Alt + 0187

…

After teaching students how to type the letters and symbols in Spanish, I give my Spanish-speaking students the following assignment, which gives them practice in translating and keyboarding:

"Translating Important Information (Questions and Answers)"

Directions: Type each question in English, and then type the question in Spanish on the next line. On a third line, type your answer in English with your correct information by filling in the blank. On a fourth line, type your answer in Spanish with your correct information by filling in the blank. Before beginning the next question, insert a blank line.

Direcciones: Escribe cada pregunta en inglés, y también en español en la próxima línea. Además, escribe cada contestación en inglés en la tercera linea, y también en español en la próxima línea. Ponga la información en los espacios. Antes de comenzar con la siguiente pregunta, deje una línea en blanco.

Example / Ejemplo:

What is your full name? / Cuál es su nombre completo?

My full name is Scott. / Mi nombre completo es Scott.

Begin / Empieza:

1. What is your full name? My full name is _____.

2. What is your first name? My first name is _____.

3. What is your middle name? My middle name is _____.

4. What is your last name? My last name is _____.

5. What is your address? My address is _____.

6. What is your telephone number? My telephone number is _____.

7. How old are you? I am _____.

8. What is your birth date? I was born on _____.

9. What school do you attend? I attend _____.

10. What school did you attend before coming to this school? I attended _____.

11. Do you live with your parents, other relatives, a guardian, or others? I live with _____.

12. What are their names? Their names are _____.

13. If they are employed, where do they work? They work at _____.

14. How many brothers and sisters (siblings) live with you? I live with _____ siblings.

15. What are their names? Their names are _____.

16. What languages do you speak? I speak _____.

17. How long have you been learning English? I have been learning English for _____.

18. If you have any medical problems, what are they? My medical problems are _____.

(Note to any administrator of this assignment: Students are told that they can leave answers blank if they do not apply to them or if they choose not to answer. Yet, this assignment is purposeful at the beginning of the school year for getting to know your students.)

…

Sample of "Translating Document Assignment"

Directions: Write the paragraphs in Spanish for keyboarding practice, and then write them in English for translation practice.

    Me llamo Alicia Muñoz Estudio en la Universidad de México. Este semestre estudio francés, matemáticas, historia, y biología. Hay un examen en la clase de historia hoy. ¡Qué lastima! No me gustan los exámenes.

    Me llamo Nicolás Pereda. Estudio en la Universidad de Texas. Me gusta estudiar en el laboratorio de lenguas. Aquí practico el inglés con unos compañeros de clase.

Me llamo Matilde Ortega. ¿Dónde estudio? Estudio en la biblioteca y en mi cuarto en la residencia. También estudio en el edificio de matemáticas. Allí trabajo en la computadora. Ahora estoy en el laboratorio de química. ¡Trabajo mucho!

Answer key:

My name is Alicia Muñoz. I study at the University of Mexico. This semester, I study French, mathematics, history, and biology. There is a test in history class today. What a pity! I don't like tests.

My name is Nicolás Pereda. I study at the University of Texas. I like to study in the language lab. Here, I practice English with my classmates.

My name is Matilde Ortega. Where do I study? I study in the library and in my dormitory room. Also, I study in the mathematics building. There, I work on the computer. Now, I am in the chemistry lab. I work a lot!

Note to educators: Obviously, such activities can be created for learning most any foreign language, side by side, with English.

…

Other foreign language translation activities involve the use of spreadsheets. This incorporates spreadsheet practice by keying and formatting text within the spreadsheet's cells with translating words and phrases.

By category, students are given lists of words and phrases in either Spanish or English, which they enter down column A. In column B, they provide the translation. (This is a good time to teach how to lengthen the width of cells, as it is necessary for the data entry.)

Samples of the categories of words assigned are: days; months; common words and phrases, (such as hello, good-bye, yes, no, I don't know, please, thank you, see you tomorrow, good morning, good afternoon, good evening, how are you?); common questions, (such as When? What? Where? How? Why? What is your name? What are you doing? Where do you live? Where is the washroom?); numbers; school words, (such as the subjects: reading, writing, mathematics, science, social studies, computers, physical education); supplies: (such as pencil, pen, notebook, folder, crayons, colored pencils, glue, scissors, tape, ruler, book bag); books: (such as reading book, library book, math book, science book, history book); rooms and locations in the school: (such as classroom, computer lab, office, gymnasium, library, cafeteria, washroom, hallway); people at the school: (such as student, teacher, principal, assistant principal, computer teacher, English teacher, math teacher, science teacher, history teacher, bilingual teacher, physical education teacher, nurse, secretary, janitor); things in the school: (such as principal's office, locker, teacher's desk, student's desk, chair, computer, flag, poster, chalkboard, whiteboard, bulletin board, cabinet, book case, gym clothes, pencil sharpener, entrance, exit, emergency exit); supermarket: (including the endless names of foods); clothing store: (including the names of clothes); body parts: (including ankle, arm, arm pit, back, cheek, chest, ear, ear lobe, elbow, eye brow, eye lash, eyes, face, feet, finger, finger nail, forehead, gums, hair, hand, head, hip, knee, leg, lips, lungs, mouth, neck, nose, shoulder, stomach, teeth, throat, toe, tongue, waist, wrist); and, people: (such as mother, father, sister, brother, aunt, uncle, cousin, parents, neighbors, friends, fireman, policeman, mailman, clerk, bank teller, waitress, athlete, musician, doctor, children, priest, nun, minister, pastor, first responders).

Note to educators: The spreadsheets with translated words are beneficial to the students for learning their second language's vocabulary. Therefore, it is assistive to categorize the words for the students. I also have the students sort each list of words alphabetically within a category so it is like a dictionary listing. It is an assignment worth printing out for the students so they can have the resource to study new words in their new language.

…

Sample of a worthwhile keyboarding and proofreading assignment for language classes due to the content.

"Proofreading Assignment"

Directions: Rewrite the following paragraphs without errors. The errors may be in spelling, capitalization, grammar, or punctuation.

The paragraphs:

    These days, it is smart to no more than one language. In the United State, for example, it is good to no English and Spanish. The obveous advantege to knowing these two languages is that many people in our country speak at least one of these two languages. So, in our area, if you can speak English and Spanish, you can spoke to just about anyone who lives in the area. Also, if you can speak more than one language, you are gonna have a better chance of getting a good job. In current times, many emplolyer's preffer to hire someone who can Speak English and Spanish. In particuler, if you are wanting to get hired in a job where you must communicate with the public, you will have an advantage if you speak more than one language. For example O'Hare Airport hires many translators from around the world. Wordly travelers pass threw the airport every day of the year.

    Another reason people learn a second language is cause its fun to learn another language. In the past, many students have had a grate time learning Spanish and other languages, such as France. Learning French is a smart thing to do since many of our Canadien nieghbors who live north of the United State speak French as well as English.

    So, when you're looking for fun classes to take in high school and collage, you might concider learning a new language. Besides learning the language, the teacher will probly teach you about the countrys culture, to.

Note to educators: I create proofreading assignments with the intentional errors in a word processor that does not automatically correct spelling and grammar errors by default, as Microsoft Word does. It is easier to create without the errors automatically corrected. Additionally, I have students do the assignment in a word processor that does not automatically correct spelling and grammar, as I want the students to correct the document's errors without assistance. This proofreading assignment was created in Microsoft's My Notebook program.

…

Remind students the benefits of learning foreign languages, which include: learning a foreign language enhances one's brain power for learning other areas of academics; learning a foreign language makes one more conscious of his or her first language and thereby improves his or her first language in terms of words, vocabulary, grammar, conjugation, sentence structure, and comprehension; learning a foreign language greatly improves one's job opportunities; learning a foreign language creates opportunities for communicating through speaking with and writing to others who know the language; learning a foreign language introduces one to another culture differing from his or her own; and, learning a foreign language improves one's memory and cognitive ability, which results in achieving higher scores on standardized exams in reading comprehension, and vocabulary.

Music and Song

Whether an educator is musically adept or not, listening to recordings of music and songs, as well as reading about them, can be educational. Beyond the development of listening skills involved, song lyrics can be read, analyzed, and assigned to be written by the students. A benefit of teaching through the recordings of songs is that it can inspire and motivate reluctant reading and writing students. Students who do not readily connect with books or articles may very well connect to the sound of music, especially if the student is familiar with the song or the singer of the recording.

Find song lyrics that have a theme, a message, or that are an example of good writing with its imagery and creativity. Many well-written songs have a spoken rhythm and rhyme that demonstrate how good the properly constructed words feel and sound when read aloud or sung. Point out, or have students find, various writing and poetry elements within the lyrics.

Have students listen to songs that tell a story, and then have them write a brief summary of what the song's story is about to be sure they are comprehending the content. In the old days, story songs were called ballads, which means searching for ballads may help an educator find some good story songs. Ballads were often popular as show tunes and followed a distinct format of the song's story events being in the verses and the song's emotions expressed in the chorus.

In more recent times, the term ballad has diminished in use. Yet, story songs have remained through the years. Many country and folk songs that have been popular in the memorable past tell stories, such as "The Gambler" by Kenny Rogers. The symbolism is exemplified with the playing cards referenced in the chorus. Have students listen to "City of New Orleans" by Willie Nelson or Arlo Guthrie. This lyric written by Steve Goodman is a great story song. Ask students who (or what) is telling the story. Good listeners in your class will catch the line in the chorus of the song that reveals "I'm the train they call the City of New Orleans." Naturally, it is also a good time to teach personification. Point out the imagery and locations in the lyrics as the City of New Orleans train travels from Kankakee, Illinois, to Memphis, Tennessee, and on to New Orleans, Louisiana. The impeccable chronology in the lyric is a writing lesson in itself. Another story song filled with detailed descriptions as well as mystery is "Ode to Billie Joe" by Bobby Gentry. The mystery being why Billie Joe McAllister jumped off the Tallahatchie Bridge. Gentry's first-person narrative demonstrates the power that unanswered questions often have in a writer's creative writing.

"A Boy Named Sue" by Johnny Cash, "In the Ghetto" by Elvis Presley, as well as Harry Chapin's "Cat's in the Cradle" and "WOLD" are story songs with messages. Of course, other musical genres also have story songs, such as the rhythm and blues recording of "Papa Was a Rolling Stone" by the Temptations and "(Sittin' On) the Dock of the Bay" by Otis Redding.

A couple of well-crafted story song lyrics that I suggest only using for adult, college-aged students are Billy Joel's "Piano Man" and the Eagles' "Hotel California." The Eagles' song lyric makes an interesting study as it is like a movie in that each verse is a different scene about the haunting experiences the first-person narrator of the song had at the mythical hotel. Furthermore, Don Henley, one of the three writers of the song, has said the song symbolizes the mythical adventures that are found in Beverly Hills, California.

While most story songs are allegedly fictional, some are true stories. Analyzing lyrics of songs about true stories can be educationally extended into a study of the story. Like other detailed story songs, these recordings are usually lengthy. One such song is "The Wreck of the Edmund Fitzgerald" by Gordon Lightfoot. Another is Don McLean's "American Pie," which has truth in its symbol-laden lyric. While being taught the element of symbolism in writing, students would need to read or be told the meanings of the lyrical symbolism in order to understand the song's history. In 2015, 43 years after the recording was number one on Billboard's national music charts, McClean released some but not all explanations of the lyrics' content. Though Billy Joel's "We Didn't Start the Fire" is more of a social commentary than a story song, it could be used as a historical review of a four-decade time span from 1949 to 1989. The following YouTube video link is an excellent accompaniment to properly understanding the song's rapidly delivered lyrics: https://www.youtube.com/watch?v=cDPnsTRAvIM.

Novelty songs, as humorous songs are sometimes called, are often entertaining due to the story line. They became popular in the 1920s and 1930s, and then had a resurgence in popularity in the 1950s and 1960s. Regardless of the time in which the songs were popular, many of them display entertaining storytelling and can be found on YouTube.

Creatively, an educator can incorporate novelty and other short story songs into lessons for the creative, entertainment, and historical value as well as for vocabulary development. "King of the Road" by Roger Miller, "Convoy" by C.W. McCall, "King Tut" by Steve Martin, "Monster Mash" by Bobby "Boris" Pickett, "Grandma Got Run Over by a Reindeer" by Elmo and Patsy, and "Hello Muddah, Hello Faddah (A Letter from Camp)" by Allan Sherman, which is set to the ballet "Dance of the Hours" by Amilcare Ponchielli, should work.

In addition, it might be enjoyable to have the students listen to "Puff, the Magic Dragon" (or simply titled "Puff") by Peter, Paul, and Mary, and then ask students to figure out why the song was temporarily banned from radio airplay approximately 50 years ago. The writing of the song and the public's reaction to it, whether right or wrong, make a fascinating story in itself. Incidentally, the writers of the song, Peter Yarrow and Leonard Lipton, have denied that the song is filled with symbolism referencing illicit drugs of the 1960s. Respectfully, Yarrow gave Lipton half of the writers' credit because Yarrow based the song lyric on a poem written by Lipton. In a change of the times, of course, marijuana is no longer illegal everywhere.

Many interesting points can be lifted from the story behind the writing of some songs, which can be listened to and read about on the Internet. If one likes the idea of using short-story songs for listening, reading, and creative inspiration, there are hundreds on YouTube as well as other locations, including Facebook video posts, on the Internet.

War, protest, and peace songs often have powerful and controversial messages that can be analyzed for their content as well as for their time in history. One such controversial but very popular song is "War" by Edwin Starr, as it was a number one song on Billboard's national record chart during the Vietnam War. Peace songs that are inspirational with powerful lyrics include "Imagine" by John Lennon, Julie Gold's song titled "From a Distance" as recorded by Bette Midler, and "Peace Train" by Cat Stevens (Yusuf).

Of course, patriotic songs, such as "The Star-Spangled Banner," are good choices for listening, for analyzing its lyrical content, and for studying its historical value. Furthermore, it is usually easy to find a contemporary recording artist, of whom students are familiar, to demonstrate the singing of the patriotic songs on YouTube. For example, Beyoncé performed the National Anthem and Kelly Clarkson performed "My Country 'Tis of Thee" at President Barack Obama's second inauguration in 2013. Many songs, songwriters, and recording artists, as well as recording artists' performances, have interesting backstories that can make for interesting reading. For example, there was controversy regarding Beyoncé allegedly lip-synching at President Obama's inauguration. Additionally, there are many stories connected to the historical Woodstock Festival in 1969.

It may be interesting to have students find and study songs that reference or are about famous places and people. Examples of songs referencing places include "Chicago" and "New York, New York" by Frank Sinatra, "Brooklyn Roads" by Neil Diamond, and "God Bless the U.S.A." by Lee Greenwood. Songs about people who students could possibly study include "Missing You" by Diana Ross, which is a tribute to Marvin Gaye that was written by Lionel Richie, the Commodores' recording of "Nightshift," which is a tribute to Marvin Gaye and Jackie Wilson that was written by Walter Orange,

Dennis Lambert, and Franne Golde. "Abraham, Martin, and John" by Dion, which was written by Dick Holler as a tribute to Abraham Lincoln, Martin Luther King Jr., John F. Kennedy, and Robert F. Kennedy who were four assassinated American icons of social change. Elton John and Bernie Taupin wrote "Candle in the Wind" originally to honor Marilyn Monroe in 1973 and then rewrote the song as a tribute to Diana, the Prince of Wales, in 1997. John and Taupin also wrote "Philadelphia Freedom" for Billie Jean King. Finally, one of the most talked about songs that is about people in the past half-century is Carly Simon's "You're So Vain," in which Simon has finally given some details including the revelation that the song is about three people, though she only reveals actor Warren Beatty's name. If you don't think your students would be interested in any of these people, consider "Santa Claus Is Coming to Town." The list of interesting songs about famous places and people goes on and on.

Beyond the writing element of symbolism mentioned above, many songs have alliteration in their titles and lyrics, such as "Bad Blood," either the old school recording by Neil Sedaka and Elton John or the more contemporary song "Bad Blood" recorded by Taylor Swift. This is a good time to teach that songs can be copyrighted but song titles cannot be copyrighted, and that is how there are two or more completely different songs with identical titles. Consider the content lesson as well as the alliteration of the p-sound in Joni Mitchell's "Big Yellow Taxi" as she sings, "They paved paradise and put up a parking lot."

Inspirational songs may be a worthwhile listen for students. Inspirational songs cover a wide range of musical genres, including the songs "Let It Go" (from "Frozen") by Idina Menzel, "Don't Stop Believing" by Journey, "What a Wonderful World" by Louis Armstrong, "Happy" by Pharrell Williams, "Don't Worry, Be Happy" by Bobby McFerrin, "Beautiful" by Christina Aguilera, "Roar" by Katy Perry, and "Stronger (What Doesn't Kill You)" by Kelly Clarkson.

Again, most any song you can think of can be listened to online at YouTube.com. Often, music videos have the lyrics appear along with the recording, which makes it easy for students to clearly consume the songs' lyrics. At times, when the video has the lyrics, there are no images or simply one still image. I like using these videos because the visuals in some videos distract a viewer from concentrating on the lyric.

Lively or rhythmically uptempo music is a good addition to the short computer breaks given to students, as students need to get up, move a round, and get their eyes off the computer screens occasionally. While such songs as "Happy" by Pharrell Williams, "We Got the Beat" by the Go-Go's, and "I Would Die for U" by Prince may work, I prefer instrumental recordings. Recordings that may work include "Wipe Out" by the Sufaris, "Whipped Cream" by Herb Alpert and the Tijuana Brass, "Star Wars Theme/Cantina Band" by Meco, "Tequila" by the Champs, and "A Fifth of Beethoven" by Walter Murphy, which introduces them to a classical piece. Hearing the introduction of an uptempo instrumental recording could become the students' unspoken cue that it is time to get up and stretch for two-to-four minutes before returning to work.

Lastly, music can be taught through a song such as "Do-Re-Mi" (from the "Sound of Music") by Julie Andrews.

…

Create a "Music Dictionary"

Give students a list of basic music terms, and have them define the words. Such music-related word lists can include: music, song, verse, chorus, vocal, instrumental, choir, orchestra, band, a cappella, piano, percussion, woodwind instruments, brass instruments, country music, rock and roll, rhythm and blues, hip hop, and classical music.

Additionally, integrate with the computer class students' music teachers by staying informed about the units being studied in music class. Beyond supporting the music class lessons with potential reading materials on the Internet, create word lists that have terms related to the music unit.

…

Researching and writing about various genres of music, famous songs and their content, songwriters, recording artists, and musical instruments may be motivational and inspirational to the many students who love music. Beyond educational, music history is interesting to many.

…

"Recording Review Assignment"

Have students listen to a recording of a very popular song and have them write a review. The student's review should include comments about the music, the lyrics, and the reasons why he or she believes the song has been successful. Is it the song's lyrics, the music, the recording artists' performance, or a combination of these elements? The writing can conclude with the student's personal opinion of the recording, which reveals whether or not they have enjoyed listening to the recording. The students' reactions to the recording will give the educator valuable information as to the types of recordings to use in class in the future. Interesting suggestions for this assignment could include "The Lion Sleeps Tonight" by the Tokens and "Na Na Hey Hey (Kiss Him Goodbye)" by Steam, as there has been public debate as to the true value of the song versus the performers' interpretations of these songs.

Another activity for written reviews is the writing of reactions to songs' various performances by different recording artists. For example, I have students listen to "Killing Me Softly with His Song" by Fugee and Roberta Flack. Then they write a comparison. Giving background information about the song and its artists can be interesting to the students. The content of the song's lyrics has a backstory. Background stories are easily found in Wikipedia and other music websites. Select materials for this activity that are respected. Students learn that "Killing Me Softly with His Song" was written in 1971 and that Flack's version was popular in 1973. To earn the students' respect for the earlier recording, they are informed that Flack won the Grammy for "Best Female Pop Vocal Performance" and the record won "Record of the Year." Additionally, Fugee won the Grammy for "Best R&B Performance by a Duo or Group with Vocal" for their recording 23 years after Flack won.

Another good song for comparative performance purposes is "The Sound of Silence," a folk-rock song written by Paul Simon. The background of this song is mostly about its initial failure, as its initial failure teaches one to 'never give up' or to 'never say never.' When Simon and Garfunkel recorded the song acoustically in 1964, it was a failure. The singing duo disbanded, possibly never to be heard of again. The next year, without the singers' knowledge, the record producer remixed the song and overdubbed the electric guitar and percussion, which is heard in the popular version of the recording. It is common knowledge that Simon didn't like what the record company had done to the song. Yet, by January of 1966, after the alterations to the recording, Simon and Garfunkel saw their song on top of Billboard's national pop music charts. After explaining the National Recording Registry to students, their respect for the recording is earned by informing them the song was added to the National Recording Registry in the Library of Congress in 2012 for being "culturally, historically, or aesthetically important." This recording is compared to the version by Disturbed, a hard rock band from Chicago. The difference between the two presentations of the song are striking. It shows how a singer can stylize a performance to make an old song new again, just as David Draiman, the lead singer of Disturbed, has done with his powerful performance of "The Sound of Silence." Beyond the interesting comparisons of the two versions of the song, the lyrics make a very worthwhile study for students. Videos of the song displaying the lyrics are available on the Internet.

…

"Art Review Assignment"

Students can also be shown famous artwork and asked to write reviews of the art you present to them, including what they feel the artist's intent and purpose was in creating the works. Like the music people, they could be assigned to read and write about famous artists.

...

Playing soothing instrumental music in the background in a classroom, even classical music, can have a calming and quieting effect. It can accompany writing time well. At first, students may find it unusual but not necessarily interfering. Within a short time, the sound becomes as much a part of the classroom as anything else that is a constant. The benefits of studying to music include the notion that the right music can relax one's mind while decreasing distractions from voices and noise. Music can also improve one's focus and increase one's concentration.

...

The best method of learning to perform musical instruments involves hands-on experiences with the instructor present. However, when in-person teaching is not possible, technology can be assistive through readings, photographs, and videos that are available on the Internet. Additionally, when in-person musical instruction is not an option, technology programs such as Zoom, an online audio and web conferencing platform, should be considered. Students involved with musical performance should be encouraged to practice their instruments.

...

"Mondegreen Activity"

Using recorded songs, the need for speaking and singing clearly can be demonstrated. During breaks during lengthy community college English as a Second Language and Developmental English classes, I have played portions of recorded songs for students and asked them to tell me what they hear. As they struggle to decipher the words, I assert that singing, like speaking, needs to be clear. I have played the chorus of "Bad Moon Rising" by Creedence Clearwater Revival. Depending on the quality of the recording and the system on which the recording it is played, some believe lead singer John Fogerty is singing, "there's a bathroom on the right" instead of "there's a bad moon on the rise." A classic misunderstood lyric is Jimi Hendrix's "Purple Haze" in which people hear him sing "'scuse me while I kiss this guy" instead of "excuse me while I kiss the sky." An internet search for misunderstood song lyrics will give a person many more examples of misunderstood, recorded song lyrics. Incidentally, there is a word for this. When a word or phrase is misheard and given a different meaning in a song or spoken poem, it is called a mondegreen. A mondegreen is also called an oronym. An example of an obvious oronym is confusing "ice scream" for "I scream."

...

Note to educators: I have incorporated music and songs into my English, ESL, and computer courses, not only because music can motivationally be integrated educationally, but also because I love music. Music has been a huge part of my life. Students likely realize an educator's passions. One person's passions in life can inspire as well as educate others. I strongly encourage educators to incorporate their powerful personal passions into their lessons.

...

Remind the students the benefits of learning music and song, which include: a possible avenue to learning how to play a musical instrument or to become an accomplished singer; an avenue to becoming a more diverse music listener, while realizing the health benefits of listening to the right kinds of music that relax a person; the development of an enhanced mind that makes a person more intelligent; enhanced creativity; the social benefits of having a common interest with many other people who are knowledgeable of music and who enjoy music.

Technology and Computers

As shown in this text, all of the subject areas - English (Reading and Writing), Math, Science, Health, History, Geography, Foreign Language, and Music – can be integrated into educational technology while embracing computer instruction. Yet, labeling Technology as an academic subject is premature by some states' standards, as not all states and schools are fully invested with computers and other technology for their students. While this is unfortunate, it is true.

There are states, including Illinois where I am certified to teach, which assert that they have programs and services that promote and support the integration of technology into teaching and learning. However, as of 2021, according to the Illinois State Board of Education, they fall short by also asserting the following: "Although they are no longer required, we can approve public school district technology plans when needed for grant applications." In today's world, educational technology needs to be required and taught within every school's curriculum. The importance of technology has outgrown its former label of being a small part of the Industrial Arts academic area. At its most basic definition, technology is what a person uses to accomplish various tasks in his or her daily life. It is nearly essential to many.

Though Technology and Computers may still not receive the respect of other academic areas in some places, lessons regarding technology as an educational subject are offered in this section of the text.

…

Students need to learn internet usage in order to find and share information. They need to learn how to use computer applications that are used for writing documents as well as for listing, manipulating, and calculating data. Furthermore, when the need for virtual learning is necessary, operating programs on a computer becomes essential. As previously mentioned, long-distance learning can be accomplished with Zoom. Additionally, Google Classroom is one of the programs being used by many school districts. Google Classroom, a service for educational institutions including schools and universities, allows educators to enroll students in a digital class. The program has a page for students to access assignments and to find other information about their classes. Conversation between the teachers and students is possible while the teacher can track each students' progress.

To an educator, technology is crucial in that students learn in different ways, and computers and their programs give options for individualized, differentiated instruction. Technology offers options for students with special needs. It also may engage students who are often difficult to engage educationally. In current times, technology and computers are accessible at most any time and place. Downtime in education is greatly reduced because there is always something else to do and learn when there is a computer or other device at hand. A huge benefit to computer usage in education is that a school and its educators have greatly reduced paperwork when learning is on the computer, and this is better for the environment. Finally, with technology and computers, lost and forgotten assignments are usually not an issue anymore.

Of course, there are negatives, for which an educator should be alerted and can be prepared to meet. First, technology can be costly for a school. Additionally, technology breaks down at times. By educators educating themselves on basic computer maintenance, time can be saved since the technology expert in a school building, if the school has one, isn't always available at a moment's notice. In terms of students, technology can offer distractions from the learning objectives designed for them. Therefore, the monitoring of and disciplining of students is an essential responsibility of teachers to keep students from straying from the assigned educational tasks. Finally, there are health concerns if a person sits at a computer too long. Students need to take occasional breaks from their computers by getting their eyes off the screens, getting up, and moving around.

...

Sample of a "Computer Dictionary Assignment"

Students are given, or told to search for, definitions of computer and technology terms as they are encountered throughout the school year. This is an ongoing assignment and kept in their daily accessible folder labeled "Technology." Terms and definitions are added at any teachable moment. A partial computer dictionary follows.

"Computer Dictionary"

Backup is an additional file of a document saved in case the first one is lost or damaged.

Browser is needed to see the World Wide Web on the Internet, such as Google Chrome and Microsoft Edge.

CD is a compact disk on which data is saved.

Characters are the letters, numbers, and any other symbols created by the keys on the keyboard.

Caret or Insertion Point shows the location where the next character input will appear on the monitor's screen and in a document.

Computers are electronic devices that accept data, perform operations, and display the results of the operations.

Cursor is an indicator, often an arrow, which shows where the mouse is on the screen.

Data is what a computer user puts into the computer, such as files, E-mail, pictures, and recordings of songs.

Desktop is the screen on the computer.

Document is the electronic copy or hard copy, when printed, of a material produced in a word processor.

Double Space is a blank space or blank line between typed texts that have been entered into a word processor.

Download is the process of copying something from the Internet or another computer to the computer in use.

Drive is the location of files and programs. Commonly, C: drive is the computer's primary hard drive and F: drive is for saving files to a flash drive. Other common drives are for the computer to interact with CD-ROMs, floppy disks, and computer networks.

Edit is changing, deleting, or adding to text that has been typed in a word processor.

E-mail is a way of sending and receiving messages from one computer or device to another.

FAQ means Frequently Asked Questions.

File is a named document made with a computer.

Flash drive is a portable device in which computer files are saved.

Font is the type of print in a word processor, such as Times New Roman.

Graphic is a picture or an image.

Hashtag, which is also called a number sign or a pound sign, is a symbol that can be typed on a keyboard. Besides meaning number, it is used as a hashtag in social media to find terms. Additionally, it is used in writing HTML code.

Home page is the opening page on a computer; a computer can be configured to have any page as its homepage. A computer can also be configured to open to the last webpage that was open in an internet's browser.

HTML is an acronym for Hyper Text Markup Language, which is a standardized system for tagging text files to achieve font, color, graphic, and hyperlink effects on webpages.

Hyperlink is an electronic link providing direct access from one distinctively marked place in a hypertext or hypermedia document to another in the same or different document; it is typically activated by a mouse click, keypress, or by touching the screen. Besides being text, a hyperlink can be an image.

Hypertext is text displayed on a computer display or other electronic devices with references or links to other text that a user can immediately access; it is typically activated by a mouse click, a keypress, or by touching the screen.

Icon is a small symbol or picture representing something on the computer screen.

Input is data put into a computer.

Internet is computers connected through the World Wide Web for the purpose of sharing. (Incidentally, the word internet should only be capitalized when it is at the beginning of a sentence or when it is used as a noun, as it often is used as a synonym for the World Wide Web.)

Justification is putting text or images to the left, center, or right in a word processor's document.

Keyboard is a component used to enter data into a computer.

Laptop computer is a small and lightweight computer, which is designed to be carried.

Left-click is clicking on the left button of the computer mouse to make the computer do something.

Microphone is a device for converting sound waves into electrical energy variations, which amplify and transmit sound.

Modem is a telecommunication device that converts digital signals to analog and vice versa.

Monitor is an output device on which computer information is displayed.

Mouse is a small, handheld device moved over a flat surface for the purpose of moving the cursor on a computer screen.

Password is a secret code for protectively keeping data from others.

Retrieve is putting a previously saved file on the computer screen.

Right-click is clicking on the right button of the computer mouse to make the computer do something.

Save is the method of creating a file to keep a document or other type of computer creation.

Software is instruction that tells the computer what to do, which is developed by programming languages.

Spam is an abbreviation for "sending particularly annoying messages," which is basically unwanted messages sent in e-mail.

Speaker is a device that releases a computer's sounds.

Task bar is a bar on the screen that reveals the programs that are either open or available on the computer.

URL is the address bar of a computer's Internet.

Virus is usually software that infects and can cause damage to a computer.

Webcam is a video camera that inputs to a computer that is connected to the Internet. The video's images can be viewed by internet users and it's sound can be heard by internet users.

Word processor is a software program capable of creating and printing typed documents, which can be saved in a variety of file types, such as a document file, a text file, and an html file.

WWW or World Wide Web is linked computers from around the globe.

Note: Every time we add terms to the Computer Dictionary, resave the document in the Technology folder as: (YourName/ClassPeriodNumbe/Dictionary).

...

Sample of "Keyboarding Practice Exercise"

Keyboarding practice can be done with articles that are of interest to the students. I have used "Star Wars: Jedi Apprentice #1: The Rising Force by Dave Wolverton" in which the students are instructed the following: Type the following excerpts from STAR WARS without errors, as fast as you can. Save the assignment in your Technology folder as (YourName/ClassPeriodNumber/Keyboarding) when you are told to stop typing.

In the future, the students may continue reading, typing, and eventually editing the document.

Caution: Do not distribute copyrighted materials to the students unless it has been purchased or permission has been granted for educational use.

...

Sample of "Improving Typing Speed Assignment"

Directions: Type the following sentence, using the correct fingers on the correct keys, as many times as you can within the specified amount of time. After you've typed the sentence once, press the Enter Key and begin typing the sentence again. Continue until time is up.

(Every time you type this line with the correct fingers on the correct keys and without errors, you have typed 15 words since five key strokes equals one word in typing speed; the use of wrong fingers or the occurrence of typing errors decreases the words per minute score. To know how fast you can really type, use the correct fingers on the correct keys with no errors in your typing, or it isn't a true score.)

Note your score in your computer notebook with today's date when we have finished this activity.

Begin typing the sentence below when told to begin:

Typing errors occur most often when people aren't trained to type properly.

…

Sample of a "HTML: Webpage Writing Assignment"

Introductory information: HTML (Hyper Text Markup Language) is a method of writing of computer code, which creates webpages.

Writing HTML involves writing commands for the computer to understand. The basic HTML commands introduced in this lesson are HTML, TITLE, Hn (in which n is a number), HEAD, BODY, CENTER, B, U, I, P, BR, HR, UL, OL, LI, BGCOLOR.

The first code in an HTML document is <HTML> and the last is </HTML>. These two symbols nest the entire document, from beginning to end. All commands have the left arrow and right arrows on each side of the command. The code written after the text has the forward slash after the left arrow and before the HTML command. Furthermore, every HTML document has the TITLE command for the title of the webpage. That means that <TITLE> is written before the webpage title and </TITLE> is written after it. The command BODY is written at the beginning of the main part or body of the document. Hn, in which the 'n' is a number from 1 to 6, is the command to designate font size of the text on the webpage, in which 1 is the largest and 6 is the smallest. The command CENTER centers your text in the document. B is the command for bolding text. U is the command for underlining text. I is the command for italicizing text. P is the command for starting a new paragraph. BR starts a new line. HR places a horizontal line on the webpage. UL is the command to create an unordered list. OL is the command to create an ordered list that places a number in front of the items in the list; LI must be placed before each item in the lists created on the webpage. BGCOLOR="#000000" or some other six-character code gives the background color of the webpage. Several commands, such as <P>, <BR>, <HR>, and <BGCOLOR>, do not need the command rewritten after the text with a forward slash.

Directions: Study the following document as you type it into a Notebook word processor. After saving the document, it can be viewed on a computer screen's browser as a webpage titled LEARNING HTML.

<HTML>

<HEAD><TITLE>Learning HTML</TITLE></HEAD>

<BODY>

<BODY BGCOLOR="#FF0000">

<CENTER><H1><U><I>Learning HTML</I></U></H1></CENTER>

<HR><HR>

<H2>Some of the basic <U><I><B>COMMANDS</B></I></U> are: </H2>

<P>

<H3><UL><LI>HTML

<LI>TITLE

<LI>HEAD

<LI>BODY

<LI>Hn

<LI>CENTER

<LI>B

<LI>U

\<LI\>I

\<LI\>P

\<LI\>BR

\<LI\>HR

\<LI\>UL

\<LI\>OL

\<LI\>LI

\</H3\>\</BODY\>\</HTML\>

Further instructions: This is the end of codes to be typed. It is extremely important that you make no typing errors or the codes will not work. Also worth noting, the TITLE entered near the top of the code is for the computer browsers tab above the webpage and is not the title seen on the webpage. The code entered for putting a title on the webpage is done at the beginning of the BODY portion of the code. It is written as part of the text within the body. Study where the webpage's title "Learning HTML" is placed in the sample above.

Save your text file as (YourName/ClassPeriodNumber/HTML.html) in your Technology folder. The extension to your file must be .html. To bring up your webpage in your computer's browser, type the path to your file, which is "C:/YourName/ClassPeriodNumber/Technology/HTML.html.

Note to educators: HTML documents must be written and saved in a Notepad program and saved with the extension .html. There is a great deal of information regarding the writing of HTML on the Internet. To put the HTML creation in the browser, type the path to the document and the document's saved file name in the URL or address bar. A common path from a local computer to the browser may be something like "C:/users/owner/desktop/html.html." Future assignments can include students creating their own written content while adding images, changing backgrounds, and linking other webpages. I have taught after-school technology programs, in which webpage writing has been the most popular activity for many students.

…

Sample of "Extra Credit for Computer Class"

A student might raise his or her grade before report cards are issued for the current grading period by doing an extra credit report.

Directions: To earn extra credit, turn in a newspaper or magazine article that is about computers or technology. If the article is online, tell the name of the article, its author, and the URL address of the article in the report that needs to be submitted. The report is to be a written well in your own words. The first paragraph is a summary about the article. The second paragraph tells what was learned by reading and studying the article. The topic of the article should be something different from anything that has been studied in class, or it can be additional material about something studied in class.

Articles about computers and technology are found regularly in newspapers and magazines at the school library, public library, and bookstores.

The report should have at least 250 words. Type your name, the due date, and the words "Extra Credit" in the upper left-hand corner. Two lines below this information, center an original title, which should reference the content of the report. The two paragraphs will follow. Format the report as Times New Roman font and 12 cpi. The report should be done outside of class. Print a copy of the report, and bring it to class on a flash drive. Save it in your Technology folder as (YourName/ClassPeriodNumber/ExtraCredit). The deadline for turning in the extra credit report is one week from today.

…

These are sample "Tests" for Computer Class

Note to educators: Many questions are specific to the computers, technology, and programs used in the computer labs in which I have taught. Educators who want to use these types of tests need to alter the questions to accommodate their students' technological equipment, programs, and experiences.

"Computer Terms Test"

Directions: Match the term below with the correct definition or description of the term (listed underneath the terms) by placing the definition's corresponding number in front of the term.

The terms:

____Enter Key; ____Input; ____Modem; ____Internet; ____Output Devices; ____Workstation; ____Computer; ____Word Processor; ____WWW; ____Hardware; ____Cursor; ____Keyboard; ____Printer; ____Input Devices; ____Output; ____Software; ____Data; ____User; ____Characters; ____Home Row; ____Mouse; ____Monitor; ____Hard Copy; ____Flash Drive; ____C: Drive.

The definitions or descriptions of the terms listed above:

1. A global system of hypertext documents linked together by the Internet.

2. The software in the computer used for typing.

3. An electric machine that receives input from a user, processes it, and gives output.

4. A program put in a computer that tells the computer what to do.

5. What computer users put into the computer by typing numbers, letters, and other symbols or characters.

6. A person who uses a computer.

7. The key on the keyboard that moves the cursor to the next line.

8. All of the parts of the computer; any part with a cord connected to it.

9. Letters, numbers, any other symbols created by the keys on the keyboard.

10. Data entered into a computer.

11. The flashing dash, which shows where the next input will appear when typing.

12. The row of keys on the keyboard where you position your eight fingers.

13. Device that connects a computer to a phone line so that computers can interconnect.

14. Most commonly used input device using an alphanumeric set of keys.

15. Hand-held input device, which can sometimes be used in place of a keyboard.

16. Interconnected computer networks that use the TCP/IP protocols.

17. Output device that gives you a paper copy of the computer's output.

18. Output device that looks like a small television screen and shows the computer's output.

19. Things used to show the computer's output such as a printer and monitor.

20. Things used to enter data into the computer such as a keyboard and a mouse.

21. Another term for a printer's printout on paper.

22. The area in the electronic office that has all the equipment needed to perform a job.

23. Data given out of the computer that calculates a user's input.

24. A small, portable device that is inserted into a computer to save files that a user wants to use on another computer.

25. Where a user saves files when the files are being saved to the computer in use.

The answer key:

7. Enter Key; 10. Input; 13. Modem; 1. Internet; 19. Output Devices; 22. Workstation; 3. Computer; 2. Word Processor; 16. WWW; 8. Hardware; 11. Cursor; 14. Keyboard; 17. Printer; 20. Input Devices; 23. Output; 4. Software; 5. Data; 6. User; 9. Characters; 12. Home Row; 15. Mouse; 18. Monitor; 21. Hard Copy; 24. Flash Drive. 25. C: Drive.

...

"Computer Test"

Directions: Read each statement below. If the statement is true, put T in the blank before the statement; if the statement if false, put F in the blank before the statement and rewrite the statement as a true statement on a blank sheet of paper. (In front of your rewritten statements, write the number of the statement.)

Example: _____ 8. The space bar is located on the top row of keys on the keyboard.

You put F in the blank before the 8; then write on a separate sheet of paper: "8. The space bar is on the bottom row of keys."

REMINDER: Talking, looking at notes, or roaming eyes guarantees a zero/F on the test. Keep your test covered. Raise your hand when you have finished and I will pick up your test. You may do something else quietly until all tests are collected. There is no time limit on this test. If you have not completed it by the end of the class period, accommodations may be made for you to remain and complete the test.

Section One: Parts of the Computer and its Components

_____ 1. The actual computer is behind the screen a person watches while working on the computer.

_____ 2. The mouse is used to click in the computer programs; most programs require the computer user to click the button on the right side of the mouse.

_____ 3. The monitor is the mechanism that looks like a television screen.

_____ 4. A keyboard is essential to working most computer programs, especially programs where typing is involved, such as in a word processor or a spreadsheet.

_____ 5. Flash drives are used for saving files and allowing computer users to move from one computer to another with their saved files.

_____ 6. Flash drives can be delicate and need to be treated with care, as they can be damaged, making it impossible for a user to retrieve his or her files in the future.

Section Two: Opening and Closing the Computer and its Programs

_____ 7. The computers have the WINDOWS 10 desktop.

_____ 8. The little pictures on the desktop are called icons. A computer user should click on the name beneath the icon instead of the icon to open computer programs.

_____ 9. Before opening computers, the word 'student' should be in the 'name' box and the 'password' box should be empty.

_____ 10. If the computers are not opened with the word 'student' in the 'name box, the computers will not be connected to the network properly, and therefore some of the programs will not work until the computers are opened correctly.

_____ 11. To close the computer properly at the end of the day, close all of the computer programs, then click on the 'Shut Down' button followed by the 'OK' button.

_____ 12. Even if a computer is not shut down properly, it will start without any problems or time-consuming error messages the next time it is turned on.

_____ 13. When the computer is shut down properly, the screen will have a message that says, "It is now safe to turn off your computer." Until that message appears, a person should not turn the computer's power off.

Section Three: Saving and Retrieving Files

_____ 14. Before saving a file, the proper drive must be selected.

_____ 15. If a file is to be saved to a flash drive in the computer's tower, the C: drive should be selected before saving the file.

_____ 16. If a file is to be saved to the computer, the C: drive should be selected before saving a file.

_____ 17. A: drive and C: drive are the only two drives on any computer.

_____ 18. When saving a new file, each file must have a file name that was previously used.

_____ 19. When editing or updating a file that has already been created, a computer user can save the file with its previous file name again.

_____ 20. Every file name has an extension, which usually consists of three or four letters that is placed after the dot (or period) following the name given to a file.

_____ 21. The extension of a file name is very important because it tells the computer which program to use when opening the file.

_____ 22. When saving a file, you may omit (leave out) the dot (or period) before typing the extension.

Section Four: The Keyboard

_____ 23. The home row is the row of keys where fingers should be placed to type properly.

_____ 24. The first ten keys across the home row, from left to right, are: asdfghjkl;

_____ 25. The first ten keys across the bottom row of letters, from left to right, are: zxcvbnm,./

_____ 26. The first ten keys across the top row of letters, from left to right, are: qwertyuiop

_____ 27. The space bar is used to put spaces in text being typed and should be pressed with a thumb. It should be pressed twice after a punctuation mark within a sentence, once after every word within a sentence, and twice after a sentence.

_____ 28. To capitalize one letter, the 'shift' key should be pressed before pressing the letter that is to be capitalized. The 'shift' key should be pressed with the little finger on the same hand that is pressing the letter to be capitalized.

_____ 29. To consecutively capitalize many letters, the 'caps lock' or 'caps loc' key may be pressed. Most keyboards have a light on the keyboard that shows when this key is engaged.

_____ 30. The question mark is made by pressing the 'shift' key with the little finger on the left hand and pressing the ? key with the little finger on the right hand.

_____ 31. The 'esc' key is used for moving to the next line when typing in a word processor or down to the next cell when using the spreadsheet program.

_____ 32. When using the number pad, which is on the left side of the keyboard, the 'num lock' or 'num loc' key must be on. The 'num lock' light on the keyboard shows when the 'num lock' key is engaged.

_____ 33. The 'F' keys along the top row of the keyboard are called 'function' keys and have various functions in many computer programs.

_____ 34. The 'esc' key is in the upper right-hand corner of the keyboard and is used to escape from (or exit from) some programs.

_____ 35. A character on the keyboard is any letter, number, or symbol that can be typed.

_____ 36. A computer user can delete (remove) a character that has been typed by either placing the cursor in front of a character and pressing the 'delete' key, or by placing the cursor behind the character and pressing the 'backspace' key.

_____ 37. The 'tab' key has several functions. For example, it is often used to indent a paragraph within a word processing program. Additionally, it also is used to move to another cell in a spreadsheet.

_____ 38. !@#$%^&*() are some of the symbols in the row of keys with the numbers. The 'alt' or 'ctrl' key must be pressed before typing any of these symbols in the number row.

_____ 39. Keys that are pressed once to turn a feature on and a second time to turn the same feature off, such as the 'caps lock' key, are called toggle keys.

Section Five: The Word Processors

_____ 40. The word processor with many editing features on the computers is Microsoft Word.

_____ 41. When a WORD document is saved, the extension is txt.

_____ 42. One of the word processors on the computers is the Excel program.

_____ 43. When a Notepad document is saved, the extension is txt.

_____ 44. When saving a file in the word processors, first click on the 'file' drop-down menu.

_____ 45. When saving a new file in the word processors, the second word or phrase a user clicks on is 'save as.'

_____ 46. When saving any file in the word processors, a computer user should check to see that the proper drive is selected and that an appropriate file name is given to the file.

_____ 47. Using the formatting buttons at the top of the Microsoft Word program, a computer user may change the font (style of the characters being typed, such as Times New Roman), may change the cpi (characters per inch or size of characters being typed), click on the B for bold text, click on the I for italicized text, click on the U for underlining text, and may justify the text to the center or the right or the left.

_____ 48. When text is bold, it looks like this: bold.

_____ 49. When text is italicized, it looks like this: italics.

_____ 50. When text is underlined, it looks like this: underlined.

_____ 51. When none of the justified buttons are clicked on, text is automatically (by default) in the center of the line.

_____ 52. When text is left justified, the text appears at the left margin in the document.

_____ 53. When the text is center justified, the text appears much closer to the right margin in the document.

_____ 54. When the text is right justified, the end of the text is at the right margin of the document.

_____ 55. To format text, a computer user may either set the formatting buttons and features before typing the text and then turn them off after typing the text, or a computer user may type the text, highlight it, and then format it.

_____ 56. In WORD and many other Microsoft programs, a computer user may click on the minus sign located near the upper right corner to minimize the program.

_____ 57. In WORD and many other Microsoft programs, a computer user may click on the two tiny overlapping windows located near the upper right corner to close the program being used.

_____ 58. To exit (or get out of) the word processing programs as well as many other Microsoft programs, a computer user may either click on the 'file' drop-down menu and the word 'close,' or may click on the X located near the upper right-hand corner of the program.

Section Six: Spreadsheets

_____ 59. The name of the spreadsheet program is Excel.

_____ 60. The small rectangular boxes on the spreadsheet are called cells.

_____ 61. The boxes going down are called rows.

_____ 62. The boxes going across are called columns.

_____ 63. The columns are labeled by a letter and the rows are labeled by a number.

_____ 64. The name (or address) of the first rectangular box in the upper left-hand corner of the spreadsheet is A1.

_____ 65. In the spreadsheet program, formulas are used to calculate the math.

_____ 66. In the spreadsheet program, the formula for adding cells A1 through A5 is: =SUM(A1:A5).

_____ 67. In the spreadsheet program, the formula for averaging cells B10 through B50 is: =AVE(B10;B50).

_____ 68. Unlike WORD, which is the word processor program, a computer user may not format characters in the spreadsheet to be bold, italics, underlined, different cpi (characters per inch), or different font styles such as Times New Roman.

Section Seven: Internet

_____ 69. The purposes of the Internet in schools are for educational reading and research as well as for supplementing (adding to) the materials being taught in the classrooms.

_____ 70. Google is an internet browser.

_____ 71. WWW, three letters commonly seen in website addresses, stands for Wonderful World Web.

_____ 72. There is only one search engine on the Internet. It is called Yahoo. It is used to search for websites that will have information on many different topics.

_____ 73. Many internet addresses begin with the following characters: ptth://.

_____ 74. An internet address must be typed in the location box (sometimes called a URL box or an address box) near the top of the Internet browser's screen correctly or the site will not appear on the screen. A typing error like forgetting to put a period in the correct place will cause the website to fail.

_____ 75. After typing in an internet address correctly in the 'location' box, the Internet user can press the 'enter' key to get to the website.

_____ 76. If an internet site is slow, it most likely means that it either has too many visitors at the present time or the site was poorly constructed with too many graphics to be loaded on it quickly. In either case, an internet user can easily stop the loading of the slow site.

_____ 77. If internet users want to go back to the last page they saw on the Internet, they have to type in the Internet address of that last page again in the 'location' box and press the 'enter' key.

_____ 78. There is no way that someone can see where an internet user has been on a computer.

_____ 79. In a webpage, when an internet user moves the mouse pointer over hypertext or a linked graphic, the Internet user can click on the text or the graphic and go to another place (such as to the top of the current page, another page within the current site, or to a totally different website).

_____ 80. The text designed for an internet user to click on to go elsewhere is called hypertext or hyperlink. Though not always, this text is sometimes underlined, bold, or in different color than other text on the webpage.

Section Eight: HTML

_____ 81. HTML stands for Hypertext Microsoft Language.

_____ 82. An HTML file must be saved with the extensions doc or txt, or the file will not come up on the computer's internet browser.

_____ 83. HTML is computer code used to write webpages for the Internet.

_____ 84. If an HTML file is saved properly with the extension html, the file will load on the Internet browser.

_____ 85. Angled brackets, < and >, must be placed before and after every HTML code a webpage writer writes when producing a webpage.

_____ 86. The first code on every HTML document is <HTML> and the last code on every HTML document is <HTML>.

_____ 87. The title that a webpage writer wants on the top of the browser (not on the actual internet site webpage, but on the tab) should be nested between the TITLE code and HEADING code, just as the following code will give the title to a site called MY WEBPAGE: <TITLE><HEAD>MY WEBPAGE</HEAD></TITLE>

_____ 88. The forward slash in front of the command in the closing angled bracket, such as the forward slash in the </BODY > code, is not necessary.

_____ 89. <B> should be placed just before text the webpage writer wants bold and </B> should be placed after the text.

_____ 90. <I> should be placed just before text the webpage writer wants italicized and </I> should be placed after the text.

_____ 91. To insert a line break in the text of a webpage, a webpage writer must put the code <BR>. This code does not need an end tag, such as </BR>.

_____ 92. To move webpage text down three spaces, a webpage writer must enter the code <P>. This code does not need an end tag, such as </P>.

_____ 93. The background color and the various text colors are based on a six-character code, such as "#000000".

_____ 94. <CENTER> should be place just before text or images that the webpage writer wants centered and </CENTER> should be placed after the text or images.

_____ 95. The background color and the text color codes must be in quotation marks with the number sign or hashtag, #, as the first character after the quotation mark within the code.

_____ 96. The color code for black is "#000000".

_____ 97. The color code for white is "#000000".

_____ 98. Everything that a webpage writer wants on the actual webpage, including all of the text, pictures, and links, must be after the <BODY> code; the <BODY> code does not need to be closed with the </BODY> code.

_____ 99. <IMG SRC="school.jpg"> is a code that should link to a picture file saved as school.jpg.

_____ 100. <A HREF="http:amazon.com/ScottPaulsonBooks"> SCOTT PAULSON BOOKS</a> is a code that should link to a web site called SCOTT PAULSON BOOKS. HREF means hyperlink reference.

Answer key:

The following numbered statements are TRUE (T): 3-7, 10-11, 13-14, 16, 19-21, 23-26, 29-30, 33-37, 39-40, 43-47, 52, 54-56, 58-60, 63-66, 69, 74-76, 79-80, 83-85, 87, 89-91, 93-96, 99-100. Consequently, all other 37 statements are FALSE (F) and should be rewritten as a true statement.

Note to educators: Some of these test entries are specific to the computer labs and applications I used with students. Therefore, alter questions as needed to be appropriate for your students and the technology they use.

…

Remind the students the benefits of learning technology, which include: technology can help a person learn about many different topics; using technology such as laptops, tablets, and cellphones has been found to make learning more engaging and enjoyable; beyond the academics learned through technology, one can learn life's skills; technology allows a person to see and do things which helps him or her remember; knowing how to use a computer and other technology devices keeps people connected; technology can eliminate personal boredom; and, learning technology prepares a person for the future in terms of employment opportunities and more.

More

A great deal of paperwork is involved with teaching computers and technology. In this section, I share some of the many documents I have created. Some of the documents satisfy administrative requirements at the state, local, and school level. Other documents I find helpful in communicating with students, parents, my superiors, and fellow-educators.

…

For students and their parents or guardian, I created a written "Agreement" to be signed and dated by the students on their first day in my class.

"Agreement"

Due to the delicacy and expense of the equipment used in the computer lab, there must be an agreement between the school, the teacher, and the students regarding use of the computer lab. Due to the possible destruction a person could cause, the initial ground rules must clearly state that anyone who causes potential destruction to the computer or its accessories will not be allowed to use the computer lab's equipment. Being a lab course, a student who is not allowed access to a computer for lengthy periods of time will have the report card grade lowered. In addition, if a student does in fact cause destruction to a computer or its accessories, the student will not be allowed to use computer lab equipment until the student has paid for the damage. It is very important that everyone cooperate by using the computer lab with care, and thereby continuing to earn the right to use a computer. The rules, which all students are expected to follow, are detailed below.

Computer Class Rules

1. Be on time to class for initial instructions for the day's computer class activities. Keep quiet during the instruction time so that everyone will be able to hear and therefore know what to do.

2. Sit in your assigned seat and at the computer to which you are assigned. Only touch the computer assigned to you.

3. Only touch your own flash drive, and return it to the designated storage area at the end of class. Some of the work needed for your grade in this course will be stored on your flash drive. If you lose or destroy it, your grade must suffer, and you will have to pay for the replacement flash drive before receiving another one.

4. When you have a partner, share your time on the computer with your partner. Partners should have an equal amount of time to do the activities.

5. Only do the class activities you are assigned to do. Do not experiment by pressing keys you are not instructed to touch. Do not enter other programs or websites without permission from the teacher. Not doing what you are instructed to do on the computer will result in the loss of computer time and thereby will lower your grade.

6. There is no food or drinks of any kind allowed in the computer lab. This includes mints and chewing gum.

7. Keep your workstation clean for the next user. Do not leave anything behind when you leave the lab.

8. If you have a question, raise your hand, and wait for assistance. When it is time to get up, do so carefully to avoid bumping the tables that hold the computers.

9. When working with a partner or group, use 12-inch voices (low volume voices) so you won't disturb others in the room as well as students in neighboring classrooms.

10. Do your best to get a good grade in Computer Class: Be prepared for every class; on occasion, you will be told to prepare for the next day's activity by doing something outside of class; you must have your assignment completed to participate. Also, keep notes and study for every computer test and quiz.

Additionally, if you are absent, please ask about assignments you may have missed when you return. If you know you will be absent on a certain day, let me know so I can tell you what you will be missing during your absence.

Each student is receiving three copies of the "Agreement": one is to be signed and returned to the teacher, one is for the student's keeping, and one is for the student's parents or guardian.

Your grade will be determined by the following equation: 50% test, quiz, and project average and 50% class performance and participation.

Sign and date this "Agreement" to verify that you have read and understand the rules and consequences.

Student Signature _____ Date _____

Note to educators: Unfortunately, there have been times parents had to be reminded of the "Agreement" when their child carelessly caused damage to equipment. I highly recommend issuing such a document at the start of the school year.

...

For the academic classroom teachers in our school, whose students have Computer Class with me, I created an "Articulation Form."

"Articulation with Computer Classroom"

Please fill out the following information and return it to the Computer Teacher within the next week.

Teacher's Name _____ Grade ____ Date_____

Your next unit topic: _____

Beginning and end dates: _____

If applicable, please respond to the remaining questions:

What subject matter would you like supported in the computer lab in the near future?

__ Written expression (specify writings you would like addressed: topics related to…; poetry; letter writing, reports, essays, etc.)

__ Reading (Comprehension)

__ Mathematics (specify skills to be reinforced)

__ Science (specify concept)

__ Other (please be specific) _____

Please list the current objectives, if any, that you are teaching.
_____

Please be specific so that the computer lab activities can enhance and support what is being taught in your classroom. Thank you for your time to share this information.

Note to educators: I distributed this form to the appropriate teachers at least once a quarter throughout the school year.

…

For students, I created a "Your Computer Knowledge" form to be completed at the beginning of the school year to give information about the students' technology ability levels.

"Your Computer Knowledge"

Name_____ Grade___ Date_____ Class Period___

Have you used a computer or laptop before? ___ Yes ___ No

If so, how much have you used the computer or laptop? ___ A lot ___ Somewhat ___ Just a little

If you have used a computer or laptop before, what is the brand name? _____

If you have a computer you can use, describe what kinds of activities you do on the computer. (Do you use the Internet, play games, use a word processor?) _____

If you have an email address, please write it here.
_____

…

For students, I created a "Computer Class Survey" to be completed as the school year ends.

"Computer Class Survey"

Name (optional) _____ Date _____

Put a check mark if you are in ___ a Special Education Class and/or ___ a Bilingual Class

1. Of the following keyboarding and typing activities you have done this past school year, which one was best at teaching you how to use the keyboard?

___ Typing a weekly journal

___ Typing the Science Fair and Heritage/Cultural Fair reports

___ Using the typing program

___ Other keyboarding activities, such as _____

2. Of the following keyboarding and typing activities you have done this past school year, which one was the worst at teaching you how to use the keyboard?

___ Typing a weekly journal

___ Typing the Science Fair and Heritage/Cultural Fair reports

___ Using the typing program

___ Other keyboarding activities, such as _____

3. Of the following keyboarding and typing activities you have done this past school year, which one did you enjoy the most?

___ Typing a weekly journal

___ Typing the Science Fair and Heritage/Cultural Fair reports

___ Using the typing program

___ Other keyboarding activities, such as _____

4. Of the following software programs, which one(s) taught you the most? (Check no more than 3)

Note to educators: List the educational programs used on the computers throughout the school year.

5. Of the following software programs, which one(s) taught you the least? (Check no more than 3)

Note to educators: List the educational programs used on the computers throughout the school year.

6. Of the following software programs, which one(s) did you enjoy? (Choose as many as you want)

Note to educators: List the educational programs used on the computers throughout the school year.

7. Think about how much you learned from doing each one of the following activities this past school year. Put a number in front of each activity, from 1 to 7 – 1 being the activity that taught you the most, and 7 being the activity that taught you the least.

___ Journal Writing and other Creative Writing Activities, such as poems, stories, song lyrics

___ Writing reports and educational documents, such as the Science Fair report, the Heritage and Cultural Fair report, and the Computer Dictionary

___ Keyboarding/Proofreading/Spell checking activities in the word processor

___ Spreadsheet activities including the creation of graphs and charts

___ Reading documents from the Internet

___ Research/Searching for information on the Internet

___ Educational Programs/Games, including the keyboarding program

If you have any comments, please write them here:

Note to educators: List, in general, as many different types of activities as your students do throughout the course and distribute the survey near the end of the course.

…

For substitute teachers, I created the document titled "Notes for the Substitute Teacher"

"Notes for the Substitute Teacher" begins with the following statement: "Please read the following information to assist you in having the best day possible during my absence." Next, I have a detailed schedule from "8:00 AM – when the bell sounds, teachers should be in the hall to supervise as students enter the building" to "8:05 to 8:41, is First Period, which is Plan Period" to "8:44 to 9:23 is Second Period, which is Eighth Grade Computer Class," etc. I give specific instructions for lunch period because there are specific duties that need to be done. I assert, "11:32 to 12:02 is Sixth Period, which is Lunch Period. At the end of the Lunch Period, by 12:02, teachers are required to go to the Cafeteria and escort the Seventh Period Class from the Cafeteria to class. A student advisor will announce that the class should line up at the door to meet you."

I also include the following in my notes:

Where are the necessities??? The daily plans are placed on the teacher's desk. Please follow today's plans. If there are activities that involve the students' flash drives, they are located on the table next to the cabinet. Please remind students to return them at the end of the class period. Seating charts are also on the teacher's desk, placed in the Lesson Plan folder's left-hand pocket. Student Passes for students who need to leave the room and Student Referral forms for students who may have discipline problems are located in the packet. If today's plans include any handouts, they are located on the table where my computer is located (Computer #10).

If a student is sick and asks to go home, they must answer 'yes' to the following questions: Are you sick enough to go home? Is there an adult who can pick you up and take you home? If they don't answer affirmative to both questions, strongly encourage the student to stay in class because our school does not have a full-time nurse and students will be sent back to class.

Please, as time permits, leave me a note telling what was or wasn't covered today in relation to the lesson plans.

Steps to be taken in case of fire or other disasters are located on the wall near the inside of the classroom door. (For a Fire Emergency or drill, exit with the students out the back door, go down the hill, and line up at the tree at the bottom of the hill, as every class has an assigned location. For a tornado emergency or drill, the class goes out of the classroom and into the hallway, turns right, and locates between the lockers in front of Room 22, which is a short distance down the hall, as ever class has an assigned location.)

If you and the lesson plans don't get along well, allow the students to do make-up work, if they have any to do. Otherwise, have them enter an educational game for the period. These applications are in each computer's "Student Apps" folder; the students know how to open the programs. Please monitor the students to make sure they are not abusing the computer lab equipment. If anyone is, write a referral and send the student to the office.

If you have any technology concerns that need to be addressed immediately, please call the office by the intercom on the wall, which is located near the front door, and ask for the school's tech specialist. If you have any other questions or concerns, I am quite certain that the neighboring classroom teachers can assist.

Thank you. Have a great day!

Note to educators: When I leave my classroom every late afternoon during the school year, I put the "Notes for the Substitute Teacher" on top of my Plan Book and folder, which is located in the center of my teacher's desk. After all, one never knows when he or she may have to be absent. Though these notes are lengthy, any substitute teacher I may have had (the year I created this document) had Plan Period during First Period, and therefore had time to read the notes. Substitute teaching can be a challenging job. Being specific regarding your teaching instructions and classroom procedures should be assistive to and appreciated by your substitute.

…

"Required Documents"

A school, school district, and state may require documentation when technology is integrating into the curriculum. Documentation is also required when applying for IT (Information Technology) grants. (Incidentally, studying grant writing is strongly advised to anyone given the task of writing a grant; a great deal of information, including current buzz words that are good to insert in a grant proposal, is available online.) Following are samples of the documents educators may need to produce and possibly post in their classrooms.

…

"Technology Mission Statement"

Through the integration of language arts, mathematics, social science, science, and fine arts, students will discover the benefits of technology by learning the skills necessary to utilize computer applications.

As a result: Students will increase content area skills; students will apply technology skills to produce computer-generated work in a variety of formats and applications; students will apply technology skills in their content area classrooms.

Students will use the word processor to create documents that support learning in the content areas.

Students will use the Internet as a resource that supports learning in the content areas.

Students will use the spreadsheet to record and analyze data that supports learning in the content areas.

Students will use presentation software and tools to present evidence of learning in the content areas.

Students will use the database to record and analyze data that supports learning in the content areas.

Students will use educational software programs that embellish learning in the content areas.

…

"State Goals"

An educator may be required to analyze the State Goals of the state where the school is located. In so doing, state goals for each goal achieved in each academic area should be listed. Examples of State Goals written for the school where I have taught include the following:

State Goal for English Language Arts: Read with understanding and fluency; listen and speak effectively in a variety of situations; read essays to one another. The activities include: reading internet and Spanish/English dictionary activities with partners; paired reading of writing assignments.

State Goal for English Language Arts: Read and understand literature representative of various societies, eras, and ideas. The activities include: reading internet activities.

State Goal for English Language Arts: Write to communicate for a variety of purposes; use the language arts to acquire, assess, and communicate information. The activities include: journals, essays, poems, letters, and content-area reports.

State Goal for Mathematics: Demonstrate and apply a knowledge and sense of numbers, including numeration and operations (addition, subtraction, multiplication, division), patterns, ratios, and proportions. The activities include: spreadsheets used in numerical assignments; math software and websites.

State Goal for Mathematics: Estimate, make, and use measurements of objects, quantities, and relationships and determine acceptable levels of accuracy. The activities include measuring anything and entering data into a spreadsheet for data analysis.

State Goal for Mathematics: Use algebraic and analytical methods to identify and describe patterns and relationships in data, solve problems, and predict results. The activities include: spreadsheet math and algebra assignments; performing equations, formulas and functions, graphic data, and database assignments.

State Goal for Mathematics: Use geometric methods to analyze, categorize, and draw conclusions about points, lines, planes, and space. The activities include: use of draw/paint programs for geometric shape lessons.

State Goal for Science: Understanding the relationships among science, technology, and society in historical and contemporary contexts. The activities include: internet readings, computer usage lessons, and learning terminology.

State Goal for Social Science: Understand events, trends, individuals, and movements shaping the history of our state, the United States, and other nations. The activities include: internet readings on our state, the United States, and other nations; utilization of social science, geography, and map software and websites.

...

"Goals and Objectives by Grade Level"

Beyond creating a "Mission Statement" and noting the "State Goals" addressed via technology education, an educator may be required to state specific goals and objectives by grade levels or ability levels of students. Following is the document created after being given the assignment by a junior high school principal:

"Internet Goals and Objectives"

All students will learn the Internet basics.

Sixth Grade Students will: learn basic internet terminology; be able to enter a website address in the location bar properly; utilize the tool bar's basic buttons, such as Back, Forward, Home, Reload, Stop; scroll website pages properly; recognize and utilize hypertext.

Seventh Grade Students will: review internet basics introduced to sixth grade and expand the knowledge through additional practice and purposeful use.

Eighth Grade Students will: review internet basics and continue to expand the knowledge through additional practice and purposeful use.

All students will understand the purpose of the Internet

Sixth Grade Students will: view a variety of teacher-selected educational and informational sites for the purpose of learning what type of information is available on the Internet; research content area topics related to the content area classes for grade-level, content area-specific reports; take notes on research found on the Internet; word process notes in simple report form; properly credit internet sources in bibliography form.

Seventh Grade Students will: continue to view a variety of teacher-selected educational and informational sites for learning what type of information is available on the Internet; access current events and information from timely sources and websites.

Eighth Grade Students will: view a variety of teacher-selected educational and informational sites for the purpose of learning what type of information is available on the Internet; understand the capabilities of internet communication by utilizing an individual email account created for participating in a teacher-selected and administration-approved online project.

All students will utilize research tools

All students will utilize teacher-selected and administration-approved subscription sites for the students' research purposes. (List the websites provided when they have been determined).

Webpages

No Sixth Grade Students' goals and objectives in this category.

All Seventh Grade Students will: be introduced to the basic components of a webpage; cut and paste text from a web site to a word processing document for saving within an appropriate graphic file and/or for printing. (Caution: Some materials have copyright laws and need to be purchased or approved for educational use.)

All Eighth Grade Students will: review the basic components of a webpage, review cut and paste of text procedures from the Internet to do a document file, and review graphic copying from the Internet; write a basic webpage in HTML format or by utilizing a program designed for creating webpages.

…

Listing computer class activities is highly recommended, as teachers may be asked what students do in the computer lab. Here is a list kept readily available for reference.

"Computer Class Activities"

Some of the computer classroom activities are:

Word processing, including journal writing (personal diary, and school diary to assist with classroom integration); poetry and song lyric writing (besides free writing, assigned themes include current events and historical people, places, and events); letter writing (friendly and business); report writing (book reports, science fair reports, heritage and cultural fair reports); computer dictionary (listing terms and their definitions); science dictionary (listing terms and their definitions); resume writing.

The word processing activities utilize spell checks; cut, copy, and paste; formatting of text features; editing; saving of documents, and organizing folders on the computer.

Spreadsheet, including timed-keyboarding scores (recorded data in a spreadsheet); students' personal expense accounts (including graph making of the data); class roster (including sorting of the data); U.S. President's spreadsheet (including sorting of the data); Heritage/Cultural Fair and Science Fair (data for making graphs and charts).

Presentation applications, specifically PowerPoint, to prepare for the students' presentations at the District's Science Fair as well as the Heritage and Cultural Fair.

Miscellaneous

HTML, which is writing a basic HTML-coded webpage in a Note word processing program.

Map, country, and state drawing in a computer's paint program.

A computer notebook in which classroom notes are written. This information includes commands needed to enter and exit the various programs used in class, the documentation of computer-technology-internet terminology, as well as maintaining a record of timed-keyboarding scores as well as test and quiz scores throughout the school year.

Note to educators: This documentation should also list the computer-based programs and websites commonly used in class.

…

"Conclusion"

Thank you very much for reading this book. It is my sincerest hope that it has given you ideas and information that will benefit you and your students. Any comments you have regarding the text and teaching are welcome. My email address is teacherpaulson@yahoo.com.

More books by Scott Paulson:

English and Spanish: The Similarities and Differences (Including an Extensive Grammar and Phonics Review), which teaches language learners about the two languages.

English to Spanish Translations for Contemporary Conversation, which translates words and phrases useful for English speakers conversing with Spanish speakers from Latin American countries, including Mexico; the text includes translations from basic greetings to vocabulary needed when discussing popular contemporary topics and occupations to the raw street language spoken and heard among Spanish speakers.

Christmas Words and Phrases in English and Spanish: Palabras y Frases Navideñas en Inglés y Español," which translates more than 400 Christmas and seasonal words and phrases from English to Spanish and vice versa, and includes the translation of popular song titles of the holiday season.

70 Life's Lessons, which has a self-explanatory title and is an update of his book titled *65 Life's Lessons: The Most Important Lesson from Each Year of My Life*.

Instrumentals: The Number One Instrumental Recordings from 1950 - Present, which tells a great deal of information about every instrumental recording that has reached number one on Billboard's popular music charts since 1950, including researched facts and trivia about the songs, the recording artists, and the songwriters.

My Life as a Song: The History of Recorded Music, which is a historical fiction book about the life of a popular song that was fictionally born in 1892 and is still alive in the 2000s.

My Family Won't Read My Books: About Venting Emotions, which tells the researched pros and cons involved in venting one's personal angers and frustrations, while the whimsically titled book reveals some of Paulson's personal frustrations from the past and how he has handled some of his own frustrations in life.

Food Delivery Tales: True Stories about Delivering Restaurant Food (Including How to Get a Delivery Job), a book in which Paulson tells his most interesting true stories about delivering restaurant food part-time in Chicago for several years.

Restaurant Stories, which is a book about some of the good and bad dining experiences Paulson has had through the years.

Walk – Don't Run, which is Paulson's childhood memoir including historical accuracy.

Made in United States
North Haven, CT
19 August 2022